WHY DOES JESUS MAKE ME NERVOUS?

GERALD MANN

WHY DOES JESUS MAKE ME NERVOUS?

Taking the Sermon on the Mount Seriously

WORD BOOKS
PUBLISHER
WACO, TEXAS

WHY DOES JESUS MAKE ME NERVOUS?

ISBN 0-8499-2926-1
Library of Congress catalog card number: 80-51445
Printed in the United States of America

Scripture Quotations marked KJV are from the King
James Version of the Bible. Other Scriptures are
paraphrased by the author from various translations and
the Greek New Testament.

For Lois:
The best rib this Adam ever had,
and an unnerving Christian
if there ever was one

TABLE OF CONTENTS

INTRODUCTION

Thanks, Mr. Rees, Wherever You Are!

I don't know the Reverend Wilbur Rees—only heard of him once. It was Saturday night, and I was out of "soap" for Sunday morning worship. I had spent a harried week priesting the flock, and there had been no time to prepare a sermon.

Miss Mildred Garrett, a parishioner with the eye of an eagle and the heart of an angel, must have known there would be days like this when, several weeks earlier, she had given me a box full of sermons from the National Radio Pulpit.

I have a strict code about using ideas from other preachers. If I'm going to steal, I only steal from the best, and I always give them the credit—unless, of course, I can completely reword and disguise their offerings to make them look like my own.

Anyway, as I hurried through Miss Mildred's gifts, I came across Ernest Campbell's sermon, "On Living Out of Phase."[1] Since Mr. Campbell is definitely one of the best, I decided to risk a few precious moments. It was there that I heard of Reverend Rees for the first and last time.

According to Mr. Campbell, Rees suggests that sermons ought to be rated the way movies are, so that people going to church will know what to expect. Sermons rated "G" would mean "generally acceptable to everyone." These are sermons filled with cream-of-wheat platitudes like "Go ye into the world and smile,"

9

and "What the world needs is peace, motherhood, and fewer taxes." The G-sermon is greeted as being "wonderful" or "marvelous."

"PG" sermons are for more mature congregations. They make mild suggestions for change, but they are always subtle enough to allow the preacher to change his position if challenged to do so. "PG" contain esoteric language which accomplishes two things: it lets the congregation know that the preacher has been to school, and it allows him to say, "Oh, but you misunderstood my point," if he gets into hot water.

I read a sermon not long ago which bears the distinctive mark of PG. Here's a direct quote:

> The either/or of the existential situation provides a plethora of alternatives, both specific and non-specific, when one grasps the eschatological aspect of Incarnational Christology.

PG-sermons elicit the response, "deep" or "thought-provoking."

Other sermons should be rated "R"—restricted to those who are not upset by the truth. No esoteric jargon here; the preacher tells it like it is. R-sermons usually indicate that the preacher has an outside source of income, and the people label them "disturbing" or "controversial."

"X-rated" sermons are positively limited to those who can handle explosive ideas. Sermons like this really sock it to 'em! They're the kind that landed Jeremiah in the well, that got Amos run out of town and Stephen stoned. The minister who preaches an X-rated sermon had better have his suitcase packed and his life insurance paid up. The X-rated sermon elicits the response, "shocking," "disgraceful," or "in poor taste."

Thanks, Mr. Rees! I needed that—for this book!

The Sermon Is an X!

For a long time, I've felt that we Christians have never quite caught up to Jesus' demands for discipleship as expressed in his Sermon on the Mount. It's an X-sermon! If we let it speak for itself, it's too hot to handle. It shatters too many of the myths we hold about our religious devotion and our Christian lives.

Let's face it—when we really listen to him, Jesus makes us nervous. He always has, right from the beginning.

Someone once complained to Mark Twain that the Bible was hard to understand, and he replied that he was bothered more by the parts he *could* understand than by the parts he couldn't. To my mind, Twain's statement applies perfectly to the Sermon on the Mount. The parts I don't understand don't bother me much; the parts I do understand make me very uncomfortable!

Roger Baldwin, the founder of the American Civil Liberties Union, was asked on his ninety-fifth birthday whether he considered himself a radical. He answered, "Yes, but not like you mean. I am radical in terms of the Sermon on the Mount. . . . I believe in loving my enemies. . . . I believe that the world is one country and that all men are my countrymen."

Whatever we may think of Baldwin and the ACLU, we cannot deny the truth of his assessment of the Sermon on the Mount. Perhaps men like him make us nervous for the same reason Jesus makes us nervous. To take the Sermon at face value would burst our wineskins and force us to rebuild the foundations as well as the superstructure of institutionalized religion. It would revolutionize our lives. And that really makes us squirm!

Otto Riethmueller understood this when he said of the Sermon on the Mount:

Like a magnetic mountain, it has attracted the greatest spirits with undiminished force through all the centuries. For that reason also, it has had to put up with more opposition, distortion, dilution, and emasculation than any other writing in the literature of the world.[2]

"Shocking!" . . . "disgraceful!" . . . "in poor taste!" . . . "embarrassing!" . . . "got the preacher crucified"—if these are the marks of an X-sermon, then the Sermon on the Mount certainly qualifies. It unnerves us to the point that we feel we must soften its blows; we try to turn an X-sermon into a G, or a PG, or at least an R. A glance at how Christians have interpreted the Sermon over the years attests to just how nervous it has made us![3]

The early church tried for a time to take the Sermon as a literal code, that is, as an alternative to the Jewish legalism which Jesus rejected. However, this position was soon relaxed to the point that Jesus' teachings were thought to apply only to the members of the monastic orders who lived "outside the world." Ordinary laymen were not bound to observe them.

The Reformers rejected this double standard and asserted that Jesus' commands applied to all. However, if a person could not keep them, he could always rely upon God's grace to save him. Of course, the proof of one's being under grace was his success in following the rules. If he broke them, he wasn't under grace—all of which meant that the Reformers simply resurrected the very legalism which Jesus denounces in the Sermon!

Orthodox Protestants have viewed the commands of the Sermon as gimmicks designed to drive people to despair, and so to prepare them to cry out to God for help. In other words, Jesus never intended that we should keep his commandments; he posited them in order to show us our pitiful dependence upon him. The Sermon was a set-up, pure and simple.

In the latter nineteenth century, another view emerged as an attempt to interpret the Sermon on the Mount. According to this view, Jesus was not laying down rules, either for the world or for the church. He was simply trying to get us to develop fundamental attitudes and principles for facing everyday moral questions. The last thing he intended was to give us a new yoke, after having just freed us from the yoke of the Jewish Law. Therefore, his teachings are aimed at what we should *be,* not at what we should *do.*

This approach proved very convenient. One could decide how he wanted to live and what moral conduct he wished to observe, and then he could accommodate Jesus' teachings to fit his decisions!

Albert Schweitzer gave us a new wrinkle for handling the Sermon. According to Schweitzer, Jesus meant every word he said, literally. But he thought the kingdom of God was immediately imminent. His commands in the Sermon were of an emergency nature— they applied only to the interim period before the kingdom dawned. In other words, Jesus was a deluded apocalyptic who was prescribing emergency measures for impending doom. We're not off base—Jesus was!

Taking their cue from Schweitzer, but modifying his conclusions a bit, others have claimed that Jesus' teachings in the Sermon cannot be taken seriously by those of us who have to function in the modern world. Some say they were relevant only to Jesus' time. They do not apply to the political, economic, and social realities of the present world. Given the reality of the current East-West tensions, how could we take seriously Jesus' command not to resist our enemy? Indeed, how could we seriously consider the suggestion to give to everyone who begs or the command not to swear an oath?

Others claim that the Sermon's commands are relevant only to some future, glorious time when God establishes his kingdom upon earth. In short, Jesus was giving us a preview of what life will be like in the sweet bye and bye.

Although all of the above efforts to deal with the Sermon on the Mount were conceived by sincere men and women who desired to forge out a relevant model for Christian discipleship, the fact remains that every one of them in effect is an accommodation—an attempt to take the "sting" out of Jesus' words.

I do not resist any effort to make Jesus' teachings applicable and relevant to the current situation. Indeed, I shall attempt to do that myself in the pages that follow. But I do resist the tendency to make Jesus an impractical idealist, his teachings dated and irrelevant. I strongly resist the attempt to shrug off the Sermon as untimely, to whittle his commands down to size, to take the nervousness out of discipleship.

The Big Question

Is there a way to take Jesus' words seriously without softening them to suit our own desires? Must we view the Sermon on the Mount as an antiquated set of teachings, to be taken with a grain of salt? What would happen to us as individuals and to society as a whole if Jesus' words in the Sermon were put into practice on an everyday basis? In short, what if we dared to accept his ideas as the rule instead of the exception—in our personal relationships, in international, political, and economic relationships?

I can't promise a satisfactory answer to these questions. But I know one thing for certain: in the two thousand years we've had the Sermon on the Mount, we've yet to build a society according to its specifications. Its ideas have made us too nervous. And the result is a pretty messed-up society *and* church. As I see it, we have little to lose by heeding what it says to us.

A word of warning: if you expect a new formula for Christian living, or a new system of Christian government, or a new theology, or a new economics, you will be disappointed by this book. What I do envision is an attempt to look as objectively as I can at Jesus' ideas from the Sermon and to allow them to challenge the status quo of our thinking. As best I can, I shall attempt to avoid hidden meanings and let Jesus speak for himself.

Prejudices: Mine and Yours

I cannot succeed fully in this. There is no way for us to completely divorce ourselves from our backgrounds, our culture, our teachers, or our personal biases. Someone has said: "When most of us think we are thinking, we are not really thinking; we are only rearranging our prejudices." That is more true than we would like to admit.

This is not to say we shouldn't think! Thinking is the best tool we have for assimilating God's revelations to us. I still say that we must try as best we can to strip away our subjectivity and dare to hear what God says. Before we begin, however, I need to come clean with some of the prejudices I hold concerning the Sermon.

First, I recognize that the Sermon on the Mount does not contain everything Jesus taught. We shall be using Matthew's account of the Sermon primarily, and it must be noted that Matthew arranged his Gospel around five discourses, the Sermon on the Mount being the first one. This means that several of Jesus' great themes are not treated in the Sermon. For example, no mention is made of the Great Commandment, or the meaning of

Jesus' death and resurrection, or justification by faith, or the work of the Holy Spirit, or the church, or baptism, or the Lord's Supper. In short, the Sermon is not a complete body of Jesus' thought. Its primary concern is with *the meaning of everyday discipleship.*

Matthew sets the stage for the Sermon, beginning in chapter 3, by reviewing the work of John the Baptist, the baptism of Jesus, the temptations, the call of four disciples, and the preaching and healing done by Jesus in Galilee. Matthew seems to be telling us that Jesus had been long enough at work that his followers were now a distinct group. "The time had come to make clear the meaning of discipleship and to define the teacher's message over against the teachings of the synagogue."[4]

The point: The Sermon on the Mount is not the full-blown theology of Jesus; it is his practical instruction to all who would dare to be his disciples. It is realistic and logical. It is no impractical, ivory-tower dream. Those who dare to take it seriously will change the world. That's my first prejudice.

My second presupposition is that the Sermon on the Mount is not a verbatim, once-delivered address. It is a collection of sayings and teachings given by Jesus at various times and later organized by Matthew or some descendant of Matthew's tradition.

I base this belief on several grounds. One is that the Sermon does not exhibit a continuity of thought from beginning to end; in between the Beatitudes and the parable of the two housebuilders it jumps from one subject to another without smooth transition. Another ground is that Luke has a version of the Sermon (6:20–49) which is similar but not identical. I agree with most Bible scholars that this indicates both Matthew and Luke drew from a common earlier source, and that their accounts differ because (1) they were writing their

Gospels to different audiences—Luke to the Gentiles, and Matthew to the Jews—and (2) Luke's account is probably more faithful to the exact wording of the earlier sources, while Matthew's account is designed to clarify the source material and make Jesus' intentions more understandable.

My third presupposition about the Sermon is that it is not a system of laws for the Christian. I cannot believe that Jesus was telling his disciples to simply exchange a set of old laws for a set of new laws. His mission was to set us free from the tyranny of rigid rules so that we could become what we were created to be—Christlike persons.

When Jesus came into the world, people thought that religion was a matter of earning God's love by keeping certain laws. The kingdom of God was looked upon as standing at the top of a "ladder of righteousness," and man's task was to climb the ladder until he reached the kingdom. The rungs on the ladder were the rules and practices one observed in order to earn God's acceptance.

Jesus came announcing that the kingdom of God was not "up there," but "down here"—the kingdom is in our midst! We don't have to qualify by climbing to the realm of God's approval. All we have to do is repent and believe in order to enter the kingdom.

How are we to take his commands in the Sermon on the Mount then? If they're not rules for earning God's approval, what are they? First, look at who they're for. *They are for people who have already entered the kingdom of God.* Both Matthew and Luke take care to point out that the Sermon on the Mount was delivered to Jesus' disciples. Both say that Jesus was being harried by a large crowd of miracle seekers, and that this prompted him *to turn to the disciples.* The words of his Sermon were for *them!* He could see matters getting out of hand. He didn't want a maudlin mob; he wanted dedicated disciples. He wanted to set them straight, get them to count the cost, have them understand what was at stake.

I'm saying that the commands of Jesus' sermon are not laws one must keep in order to enter the kingdom, but the guidelines one must follow *after* he has entered the kingdom! They are goals for Christians. Not ideals, mind you. An ideal is something one cannot reach, something we are apt to regard as being so remote that we couldn't reach it if we tried. A goal is something unachieved, but reachable.

God gives salvation when we ask for it. We cannot earn his forgiveness. But that does not mean we are under no obligations after we have received it. To accept the kingdom of God is to accept a new way of being, a new set of goals, *and* a new power to move toward those goals. This is what Jesus was trying to make clear to his disciples in the Sermon on the Mount.

Don't Miss This

My final prejudice or presupposition is that Matthew arranged the teachings of Jesus which comprise the Sermon on the Mount around the concept of the "kingdom of God," or the "kingdom of heaven"—both phrases can be used interchangeably, in my opinion. Throughout this book we shall keep alluding to this concept; therefore let me state its basic features. Unless you keep these features in mind, you will miss the underlying logic of the pages which follow.

First, "the kingdom of God" refers to God's sovereignty over any person or community that acknowledges him as king. The kingdom is God's rule over people. Second, the Bible speaks of the kingdom as existing in three stages: (1) *The kingdom has always existed,* since God, the Creator, is the lord of all that is. But God created us as free beings. He gave us the choice of accepting or rejecting his lordship. Our forefathers chose to reject his lordship, and God's kingdom ceased to exist for a time. (2) In Jesus Christ God brought his kingdom back into history. Therefore, *the kingdom is.* Everyone who accepts Jesus as lord has already begun to enter the kingdom. (3) However, *the kingdom is also yet to be.* A time is coming when everyone will acknowledge God as king, when his kingdom will fill the earth.

In short, the kingdom which God willed in the creation—which was delayed by our rebellion—has already entered the world in Jesus and is growing to its future consummation. From this we see the meaning of Jesus' parables concerning the kingdom. It is like a mustard seed that begins unnoticed (a babe in a manger) and grows up to overshadow all else. It is like a sprinkling of yeast in a mountain of dough, swelling and transforming the whole.

Christians are God's partners in bringing in the kingdom. This means that the Sermon on the Mount is a manual for God's partners. To transform the world according to God's plan is to reach for the standards Jesus sets forth in the Sermon. These standards may seem absurd, given our modern world, but they are the keys to the kingdom of God.

Summary

The Sermon on the Mount makes us nervous because its teachings are X-rated—in the sense that the Christian world has never dared to take them seriously. Christians have constantly pawned them off as dated, impractical, and idealistic. Instead of using them to change culture, we have allowed culture to change them. And the result is that we have yet to catch up with the world-transforming power which Jesus proclaimed.

We must attempt to hear Jesus' Sermon again, while there is yet time. We must attempt to let him speak through all of our prejudices and fears, if we are to become effective agents for the kingdom.

However, there are certain precautions that must be taken at the outset. First, we must remember that the Sermon on the Mount does not contain all that Jesus said. Its primary aim is to give us a feel for what it means to be his disciples on a daily basis, but it must be clarified and corrected by everything else Jesus taught. Second, because the Sermon is not a complete, once-delivered address, we should not try to enforce an outline of hidden meanings upon it, but let it speak for itself. Third, most of all, we should remember that the Sermon is not a new legalism. It is not a list of activities for earning God's approval, but a set of moral guidelines for those who have already entered the kingdom and are working to bring it to its consummation. In short, Jesus' commands are not requirements for entering the kingdom; they are the requirements for bringing the kingdom to the world!

> The Sermon on the Mount is directed to those who have already begun to enter into the new age and who have begun to share its new powers. It should never be forgotten that both its ethical teachings and its confidence in God are spoken in a context of salvation.[5]

One More Thing

I urge you to go no further in this book until you have read Matthew 5–7. You might then want to read it from several translations, for you may discover, as I did, that your *impressions* of what the Sermon on the Mount says and what it really says are two different things.

I have used several translations, in addition to the Greek New Testament, as the basis for this study. (The Scripture quotations in this book are for the most part my own translations or paraphrases.) I have discovered that every English version of the Bible has both strengths and weaknesses. The chief weakness is that all translations are like you and me—they cannot escape their prejudices.

At any rate, *read* the Sermon on the Mount!

QUESTIONS FOR STUDY

1. Why has the Sermon on the Mount posed a problem for Christians throughout the centuries?
2. Describe the historical attempts of Christian interpreters to "soften" Jesus' commands in the Sermon.
3. Does the Sermon on the Mount represent the totality of Jesus' thoughts on religious life? If not, what major religious themes are not included?
4. What is the difference between an ideal and a goal?
5. Is the Sermon on the Mount, as we know it, a once-delivered, verbatim address given by Jesus?
6. Why are Matthew's and Luke's accounts of the Sermon different?
7. Are Jesus' commands in the Sermon to be understood as new religious laws? If not, what are they?
8. Define the term, "Kingdom of God," and explain its three stages.
9. Where in the Bible is the Sermon on the Mount located? Give an outline of it by chapter and verse.

CHAPTER ONE

UNNERVING NOTIONS ABOUT HAPPINESS

(Matthew 5:3–12)

Unhappiness Is

A couple of years ago, the editors of *Psychology Today* sent questionnaires to fifty-two thousand subscribers in an effort to determine what makes people happy.[1] From the survey, they concluded that there is considerable confusion in America about just what constitutes happiness! Quite a few of those surveyed asked to be informed of the results; one subscriber said, "I think I'm happy; would you please verify?"

The editors were able to rule out some factors that are commonly thought to contribute to happiness. How much wealth one possesses apparently doesn't determine whether one is happy. Whether one is an atheist or a believer isn't the determining factor either. Where one lives has little to do with happiness. Sexual preference—homosexual or heterosexual—had little bearing on the results, nor did being married or single. Apparently, happiness is a matter of inward attitude—the way we regard our circumstances and ourselves.

What makes us unhappy? The survey found that much unhappiness results from comparing one's lot in life with another's: *unhappiness is wanting what I don't have but think you do have.* Many married women surveyed were unhappy because they stayed in the home and other wives worked outside the home. These "housebound" wives thought they were being deprived of independence and self-actualization. At the same time their counterparts, the working wives, were unhappy because they couldn't stay at home and "luxuriate" like the housewives did! The members of each group were gauging their happiness by what they thought was someone else's happiness.

Another source of unhappiness revealed by the survey is allowing expectations to exceed abilities. Happy people balance what they want with what they can have; unhappy people do not. *Unhappiness is wanting what I can't have.*

The survey also concluded that *unhappiness is not wanting that which I know I can have.* One of the quirks of human nature is that we pursue the unattainable and take for granted what we can obtain easily. A child loves a toy much more when he sees it on the shelf at the store than after it has been his for a week. A girl is much more alluring when her boyfriend is pursuing her than when she has been his wife for a year. I heard about an experiment with pigeons which illustrates this principle. A pigeon was placed in a cage rigged with a wooden bar. When the pigeon pecked the bar a morsel of food dropped into a pan. The experimenters learned the following: (1) If no food dropped when the pigeon pecked the bar repeatedly, he stopped pecking altogether. (2) If food dropped *every time* he pecked the bar, he became disinterested and pecked only occasionally. (3) But if there was no predictable result when he pecked the bar—that is, if the food dropped *intermittently*—the pigeon pecked like crazy!

Granted, we are not pigeons; but our nature resembles the pigeon's in this respect: what we know we can have we tend to lose interest in; what we're not certain we can have we pursue with a passion. Much of our unhappiness comes from the pursuit of that which we cannot have and the failure to appreciate that which we know we can have.

The pursuit of happiness is part of the trinity of American idealism. It's right there in the founding document, folks—life, liberty, and the pursuit of happiness! And yet, pursue as we will, most of us can't find it. When some author produces a new book on how to be happy, we rush to the nearest bookstand to buy it. We have our happy pills, happy buttons, happy hours, and happy songs. We allow Madison Avenue to create our tastes with a never-ending parade of gadgets and gimmicks designed to give us happiness. And then we must rush to the liquor or medicine cabinet to grab a happy potion in order to dull the anxiety created by our not being able to afford the pursuit of happiness!

Happiness Is?

It might help to ask, what is happiness? But that's where we get into trouble. Is it feeling? Is it having—possessing? Is it unencumbered leisure, the absence of all restraints, uninterrupted ecstasy? Is it a sense of purpose? Is it freedom from all threats? Or, as one bumper-sticker says, is it "a loaf o' bread, a jug o' wine, and yo' sweet body"?

Isn't it strange that we all know what happiness is, but we can't define it with words? Maybe our problem is that we only think we know what happiness is. Maybe we've allowed others, our culture, to define happiness for us. Then when we reach what we've been told it is, we see that it's not the real thing.

Happiness Happens

Jesus had some things to say about happiness. His ideas are contained in those eight poetic sayings called Beatitudes which introduce the Sermon on the Mount. We'll look at them in the next few pages. But I must warn you that Jesus' ideas about happiness are about as welcome in the American culture as an Arab in a synagogue. Like the rest of the Sermon, the Beatitudes are rated X in terms of acceptability; they have little to do with the "pursuit of happiness" as we commonly know it.

Before we examine Jesus' sayings about happiness one by one, it would be helpful to look at a couple of principles which underlie all of them. First of all, happiness is a result, not a goal. It's not something we search for and find; it's something that finds us while we're searching for something else.

Several years ago, my wife Lois misplaced an heirloom, a ring given her by her grandmother. We were turning the house upside down, growing more frantic by the minute, and our four-year-old daughter picked up on our anxiety. When she couldn't stand the tension any more, she blurted, "I know what! Let's look for something else, and maybe the ring'll turn up!"

Unwittingly, she had expressed an important truth about happiness: happiness turns up while we're looking elsewhere. We don't create happiness; happiness happens as the result of our pursuing something else.

This leads us to the second principle: *the "something else" which we are to pursue in order for happiness to find us is the kingdom of God.* Later in the Sermon, Jesus says this explicitly: "Seek ye first the kingdom of God" (Matt. 6:33, KJV). But this command is implied throughout his sayings about happiness.

Thus, happiness is not a treasure which we can create or uncover. It is a by-product of our seeking the kingdom of God. And remember—the kingdom of God is the full reign of God over a person, a community, or a world that acknowledges him as king.

In short, Jesus is telling us *not to seek happiness!* If being happy is our primary motive for embracing God, we won't find happiness!

We tend to forget that the pursuit of happiness can be just as idolatrous as the pursuit of mansions, Cadillacs, or careers. An idol is *anything* one substitutes for God.

Years ago I served a church where it was open season year-round on the preacher. The church had had five pastors in the five years before I came. By the end of my first six months there, I had become totally "de-mythologized"—that is, all my rosy illusions about the church's being a community where constant love and tranquility reigned were shattered.

I went to see my friend and adviser Carlyle Marney— God rest his pure heart. "I'm considering chucking it all," I told him. After I explained the situation to him, he thought for a while, and then said, "Okay, what is the dominant reason you want to quit?" "I'm unhappy," I replied. "Well then," he said, "you ought to quit! Whoever told you that you had a right to be happy? The ministry is no place for the pursuit of happiness . . . it's a place for the pursuit of the kingdom of God!"

Talking with Marney made me realize that the pursuit of happiness had become my idolatry. And I am convinced that the same is true for scores of Christians.

The Russian dissident writer Alexander Solzhenitsyn pinpointed the sickness in the American tendency to idolize happiness when he spoke at the Harvard commencement in 1978: "Even biology knows that extreme safety and well-being are not advantageous for a living organism," he said. And later he uttered another prophetic note: "If humanism were right in declaring that man is born to be happy, he would not be born to die."[2]

This is precisely the drift of Jesus' sayings about happiness in the Beatitudes. The pursuit of happiness as a goal is an idolatrous quest. There is nothing wrong with the desire to be happy. There is everything wrong with the way we often go about seeking it.

Well then, if happiness is a by-product which occurs

out of the process of our seeking the kingdom of God, how can we seek the kingdom of God in such a way that happiness will find us? In other words, what does it mean to seek the kingdom of God? Enter Jesus' unnerving ideas.

Happiness Happens to the Poor in Spirit

First, the seekers of the Kingdom, who will be found by happiness, are the "poor in spirit" (Matt. 5:3). Much has been said about what it means to be poor in spirit. To me, it means simply "not inflated in spirit." Happy are those who are unspoiled, those who don't get ruined by the self-delusion that they deserve the kingdom, those who don't pretend that they are more than they are, those who remember that they are, after all, dependent beings.

I love that scene from the old movie classic, *Quo Vadis*, in which the Roman general is making his triumphant entry into Rome at the head of his victorious legions. Thousands are screaming their accolades; the emperor is waiting to place the wreath of victory upon his head. At the same time, a slave stands in the chariot, holding a crown over the general's head and repeating constantly, "Remember, thou art only a man." Happy are those who remember that they are only mortal, perishing creatures.

This notion doesn't sit well with our culture. Happiness is supposedly reserved only for those who are able to exceed human limitations! For an athlete, happiness means breaking the record. For a parent, it means raising three perfect kids. For a writer, it's the all-time bestseller. For a preacher, it's the biggest church, with the biggest budget and the most baptisms. For the politician, it's the highest elective office in the land.

From our earliest rational moments, we are taught that happiness means exceeding our humanness. In a sense, the whole American Dream is aimed at overcoming that which makes us human. For example, our forefathers settled this land by operating on the premise that nature is the enemy to be conquered and subdued. And, of course, the premise behind this premise is that we humans are not part of nature—we are above it and separate from it, not creatures who must live in harmony with it.

Our technology, our economy, our educational system are all designed to lift us beyond our *creatureliness*. In short, the American Dream is the dream of capturing immortality by defeating nature.

Shortly after World War II, the German theologian Helmut Thielicke toured this country's university campuses to carry out a dialogue with faculties and students. In one session, he was asked to define what he thought was America's greatest challenge at the moment. He replied that the greatest question facing America was the question of how to handle suffering.[3] He noted that we Americans are possessed with the notion that we can "do anything," solve any problem, and overcome any obstacle through technology and hard work. And according to Thielicke, we *can*, save for one problem—*the problem of having to die.*

The one place where our philosophy of grandeur is vulnerable is at the point of growing old and dying. The way we're facing the problem, says Thielicke, is with illusion and self-deception. For example, when it comes to death, we simply ignore it. We shelter ourselves from it by devising "soft" words and phrases like "expiring," "passing on," and "going to be with God." We remove ourselves from the responsibility of dealing with the dead by paying the undertaker to do it. Our funeral etiquette is designed part and parcel to shut away from our consciousness the stark reality that we are mortal creatures on our way toward death.

I would add to Thielicke's analysis a couple more examples of the way we handle this one chink in the American armor. One is our passion for youth; health spas, diet programs, cosmetic companies, and self-improvement courses are booming as Americans try to deny the facts of aging and death. Another example is the recent popularity of "scientific" accounts of life after death. We have made bestsellers out of books based on interviews with persons who have "clinically died" and returned to life, and who tell us that there *is* life after death, that in most cases it is a pleasant, joyful, ethereal existence regardless of one's present lifestyle.

My assessment of all of the above is that we Americans have finally begun to realize that all of the "saviors" we embraced during the first two hundred years of our history have begun to desert us, and that we are now bent on finding a new mechanism which will allow us to evade the truth of our mortal, creaturely existence. Technology, with all of its gadgets, didn't save us; education hasn't saved us; weaponry hasn't saved us; "Dr. Soup's Super-Savior-Diet" hasn't saved us; jogging, jerking, bending, stretching, salving, soothing, pasting, perfuming, meditating haven't saved us.

And we are unhappy!

When will we hear what Jesus says to us in this first Beatitude? Happiness can never happen to us as long as we refuse to accept our finite, creaturely dependence! Happiness happens when we accept the fact that we are headed toward death, when we stop deceiving ourselves into believing that we are gods and not humans.

So the popular notion in America is that we earn happiness by exceeding our human condition—by step-

ping beyond the limits of our mortality. But Jesus'
unnerving notion is that happiness happens when we
fully embrace our finite condition and depend upon
God's grace. The people who experience God's kind of
life—the kingdom of heaven—are those who are not
taken in by their accomplishments, comfort, and ac-
claim.

Jesus' idea makes real, practical sense when you think
about it. For instance, consider what a hard task it is to
maintain false self-images. Convincing yourself that you
are something you're not is a tough exercise. You have
to lie to yourself and to others. And once you begin to
live with the illusion of self-grandeur, there's no turning back. You have to keep up the old image. You can't
allow doubts or realities to creep in.

Arthur Miller described the torture which accom-
panies the illusion of self-grandeur in his portrayal of
Willy Loman in *Death of a Salesman*. Willy is the classic
victim of the American Dream. He is out to find
happiness, which of course lies at the top of the heap in
the world of salesmanship. After achieving a measure
of success, he finds himself being overtaken by old age
and more energetic young salesmen. His family relations are in disarray; he has no friendships; his health is
failing; he has lived his entire life on the basis of
competition, which in his world means dominating
others and beating the other guy.

Throughout the play, he is haunted by the image of
Uncle Ben, his highly "successful" relative who has
made a fortune in jewel mining in Africa. Every time
Uncle Ben appears, he says the same thing: "When I
was seventeen I went into the jungle. When I was
twenty-one I came out and, by God, I was rich, boy!"

Willy dies, never having found the jewel of happiness, in the jungle of life. Standing at his grave, one of
his boys says, "I'm going to get what he was after . . ."

The other son says, "No . . . he never knew who he was."

Happy are the poor in spirit. It makes sense! Happiness never finds us while we're trying to become something we are not.

Now, look at the other side of the matter—that is, the business of being *what we are,* accepting and embracing our human limitations. How can this kind of attitude produce happiness? Does it mean that we are to go about with long faces, thinking about our impending death at every moment? Does it mean that we are to cease all efforts to overcome disease and ignorance and everything which threatens us? Is *that* what accepting our humanness means?

Not at all. Remember what I said earlier: Jesus' teachings in the Sermon on the Mount are directed toward those who have already accepted him and have entered the kingdom. In a word, he is speaking to those who have already begun to experience God's grace and forgiveness and newness of life.

If we haven't had that experience, this poor in spirit business is sheer nonsense. But those who *have had* the experience have no trouble accepting their human condition, *because they know they have a future.* They know it's OK to be human, dependent, finite, creaturely. They know that God loves them in the midst of all of their humanness! They don't have to pretend, to dominate, to exceed their finitude, to fear death and old age—"for theirs *is* the kingdom of heaven," already! And happiness finds them as they devote themselves to ushering in the kingdom with all haste.

Happiness Happens to the Mourners

Jesus' second idea about how to be found by happiness is also unnerving for our society. "Happy are those who mourn," he says. Happiness is experienced through grief—what an absurd notion! Whoever heard of such a thing?

In the common way of thinking, grief and happiness are opposites. Anyone who has lost a loved one, whether by death, divorce, or rejection, knows that there is not a greater unhappiness. And we expend a large portion of our energies in the attempt to evade grief. As I noted earlier, the American Dream is aimed at insulating ourselves from grief experiences.

And yet Jesus tied grief to happiness. What on earth could he mean when he says that happiness finds those who grieve?

Some would say he means that happiness comes only to those who grieve over their own sins. In other words, the second Beatitude is tied to the first: "Happy are those who know they are sinners (poor in spirit), and happy are those who grieve (mourn) because they are that way."

If we accepted this interpretation only, we would be going around dressed in black, with sorrowful faces. There could be no joy and celebration, only guilt and self-hatred. Therefore, I cannot accept this as the full interpretation, although I do think it is included in Jesus' meaning.

In my opinion, Jesus was saying essentially two things. First, we never begin to live fully until we have experienced grief and overcome it. An essential part of being human is facing and conquering grief in such a way as to turn it into something good. Indeed, what would we be without the grief experience? Dull, unfeeling machines, robots, whiling away our time plucking fruit from trees, with no sense of time, no challenges . . . we wouldn't be human at all! Without grief there would be no way to tell the difference between good and best or worst and better. There would be no values—no appreciation for what we have—because there would be nothing to compare it with. Happiness happens to those who have known the depths of human grief, for only they can fully know the heights of joy.

But that's not the way we tend to look at happiness, is it? In our way of thinking, happiness equals the absence of grief. Happiness is found by dodging, outwitting, and escaping every occasion of discomfort.

We even use our religion—or at least we try—as an escape mechanism. In spite of the fact that the Bible makes no such promise, many of us believe that, because we practice religion, we will be exempted from suffering and sorrow. Whenever tragedy strikes, we become embittered at God, as though he had promised us that faith in him meant an escape from tragedy. God never promised that we wouldn't suffer. He never promised to wrap us in a germ-free package. Those who claim otherwise have allowed the American tendency to evade suffering at all costs to read too much into the Bible.

So, "Happy are those who mourn" means that happiness finds those who accept their human condition as one which involves suffering, and who vow to turn it into something good. Happy are those who know that, while they cannot evade grief, God is there in the fight with them and will lead them through it to a higher ground. In a word, if you can't grieve, you can't be human, and therefore, you can't be happy.

The second thing I believe Jesus is saying is that happiness happens to those who grieve for the right things. Much of our weeping in life is for the wrong things and the wrong reasons.

I once led a group of six married couples—all faithful church-attenders and believers—at a retreat. In one of the sessions I asked each person to write down three things that were causing him grief and hurt at the present time. I instructed them not to sign their names or to describe their hurts in such a way as to reveal their identities, if they wanted to remain anonymous.

The answers were intriguing. One person, obviously a woman, said that her washing machine had self-destructed the week before, and she had been forced to go to the washateria. Another said that he had needed to sell the new car he had recently purchased in anticipation of a raise which didn't come through. Another said that the children had moved thirty miles away to another town and that he/she missed the grandchildren. Perhaps many of these people didn't divulge their real grief because they were afraid to share the intimate and personal in a forum like ours. However, even if the things some of them listed weren't their deepest hurts, they *were* hurts. Otherwise, they wouldn't have come to mind as quickly as they did.

All of this points to the fact that we often grieve over nonvital things. This is certainly true for me. For years, my most materialistic ambition in life was to own acreage in the country—a small ranch with wild game on it. It was my obsession. Perhaps because I'm a Texan, and the classic mark of respectability in Texas is to own a ranch. Or perhaps it was because all of the men in my family own ranches and I, having chosen a nonmoneymaking profession, had never been able to afford one. Anyway, I found myself yearning, dreaming, and hustling to somehow scrape up enough money to buy a ranch.

Then I found it! A beautiful three-hundred-acre plot with a mile of crystal-clear river frontage! It was a steal! I hocked my soul and body to acquire it. I had no idea how I would afford to make the payments, but I was convinced that God would provide.

The whole experience turned into a nightmare. The local county government was ruled by a militant, socialistic judge who was bent on running all of the "rich oppressors" out of the country. He wanted my land for a public park, but since the county had no money to purchase it legally, he set about taking it away from me illegally. My fence was torn down, and the county built a road the length of my river frontage.

I appealed to the state and federal governments without result. When I locked my gate, the judge sued me!

I couldn't sell the place—who would buy it! I had my life-savings invested in it. If I lost it, I would be bankrupt. For weeks I couldn't sleep. I couldn't work for thinking about it. I had all of the symptoms of a full-blown depression—even collapsed one day at work. Let's face it—I was having a grief-experience. All that I had dreamed of was shattered. My self-image, my success-image, my feelings of worth plunged to a low ebb.

As it turned out, I sold the ranch—at a financial loss but at a great spiritual and emotional gain. I discovered that unhappiness does not come from having to grieve, but from grieving over the wrong things—the things that really don't count anyway. I wanted a ranch . . . I got a ranch . . . I lost a ranch. I grieved over it and almost lost my mind and my health in the process.

Now, I'm laughing at the folly and stupidity of it all. I almost lost my soul over three hundred acres of dirt! It sounds as silly as grieving over a broken washing machine and thirty miles of road between a grand-parent and his grandchild!

Unhappiness comes from grieving over the wrong thing. Happiness happens when we grieve over the right things—that's Jesus' message to us. But, what are the "right things" over which we should grieve?

I think Jesus gives us a clue in the seemingly abrupt statement he made to those women who were weeping as they watched him carrying his cross to Golgotha. "Weep not for me," he said, "but weep for yourselves, and for your children" (Luke 23:28, KJV).

Who were the women? They were not his followers, but the sympathetic, emotional weepers who frequently shriek and blubber at the sight of any tragedy. I think the message is: *If you're going to cry, cry for the same things Jesus cried about . . . weep for that which makes God weep. Happy are those who mourn what God mourns.*

And what does God mourn? He mourns the brokenness, the lostness, the confusion of the world he created. He weeps because he would gather us to himself like a hen gathers her chicks, but we won't come. He weeps when we think our brother Lazarus is *forever* gone because he has died. He weeps as Hosea wept when the one he loved deserted him and sold herself into bondage. He weeps because we have lost our capacity to be astonished by our own sins. He weeps because we don't know a savior when we see one. He weeps because we can no longer hope in him.

In short, Jesus' message is that happiness finds us when we grieve over *that which obstructs the progress of the kingdom.* For it is this kind of mourning which God comforts. Jesus doesn't say that God brings comfort to everyone who grieves over everything; he says that God brings comfort to those who grieve over the right things. He knew full well that grief in itself does not produce happiness. He doesn't want us to be masochists, to seek pleasure in pain. He is not telling us to become martyrs and to punish ourselves. He is a realist. He recognizes that everyone inevitably experiences sorrow; and he is saying that, since we're going to grieve anyway, we should grieve over the right things, that is, the things which can be comforted by God.

A classic example of how happiness finds those who grieve for the right things is the German pastor, Dietrich Bonhoeffer, who was executed by the Nazis in 1945. Bonhoeffer fled Germany in the thirties because of his opposition to Hitler. He came to America, but eventually decided to return to his homeland because he knew his countrymen were suffering, and he wanted to suffer with them.

After returning, Bonhoeffer eventually participated in a plot to assassinate Hitler, was arrested, and executed without trial. On the eve of his death, a cellmate was inspired by the serenity with which Bonhoeffer faced the end:

> Sunday, April 8, 1945: Pastor Bonhoeffer held a little service and spoke to us in a manner which reached the hearts of us all, finding just the right words to express the spirit of our imprisonment. . . . He had hardly finished his last prayer when the door opened and two evil-looking men came in and said, "Prisoner Bonhoeffer, come with us." Those words, "Come with us," for all prisoners had come to mean only one thing— the scaffold. We bade him goodbye—he drew me aside—"This is the end," he said, "For me, the beginning of life" . . . Next day, at Flossenburg, he was hanged.[4]

Happy are those who mourn—for the right things, that is—they shall be comforted.

Happiness Happens to the Meek

Here's another unnerving idea about happiness: "Happy are the meek; they shall inherit the earth" (Matt. 5:5). For most of us, meek means weak. My five-year-old son expressed the common understanding of meekness when he got his words mixed up and called one of his timid playmates a "Casper meek-toast."

George Buttrick gave another classic caricature of meekness when he described the way many people often view the minister:

> To many he is a pathetic figure, an anachronism, a stage-joke—an offensive little man jostled by the crowd and wearing the expression of a startled rabbit. With one hand he holds a circular hat on his bewildered head and with the other desperately clutches an umbrella. The crowd pushes him from the sidewalk; the traffic shoots him back into the crowd. Some curse him; a few laugh; most are unaware of his existence.[5]

Over against these common notions, Jesus says to us, "Happiness happens to those who are meek; the earth belongs to them!" "Bull!" we say. Or, as Nietzsche said of Jesus' ethic, "I regard [it] as the most fatal and seductive lie that ever existed."[6]

In a word, we just don't believe what Jesus said! Our experience shows us—or at least we think it does—that the meek do not inherit the earth. Multinational corporations, slick politicians, thrice-married movie stars, porno-publishers, military dictators, and brutal oligarchs who call themselves "Democratic Socialists"— *they* are the ones who inherit the earth!

The American beatitude is, "Happy are the Aggressive; they shall gain controlling interest." From sports to business to churchmanship to Women's Lib to sexual technique—the watchword is, "Be Aggressive!"

There simply doesn't seem to be much hope for our hearing Jesus' third suggestion about how to be happy. The cards of our cultural biases are stacked against meekness. Perhaps this is so because we Americans have such a small sense of history about us. We are steeped in immediacy; that is, we have little feel for what has happened to those cultures of the past which disintegrated by making the same mistakes we're making. We seem to be concerned only with the present. The "Gospel according to Schlitz" is our gospel: "You only go around once, so grab for all the gusto you can—NOW!"

With this nearsighted focus, we find it difficult to understand that over the long sweep of history it has indeed been the meek who have inherited the earth. For instance, look at two Frenchmen, Napoleon Bonaparte and Louis Pasteur. When Pasteur was a boy, his schoolteacher said he was the weakest, smallest, and least promising pupil in the class. But even in his own lifetime, he was proclaimed as the greatest of all Frenchmen. On his seventieth birthday a national holiday was declared in his honor. Being too sick to attend, he sent his son to read his message, part of which was, "The future will belong not to the conquerors but to the saviors of mankind."[7]

What of Napoleon, the aggressor, who left millions homeless, in his quest for glory, but who spent his final days in exile, being poisoned by his keepers? Victor Hugo gave him his real place in history in the description of the Battle of Waterloo.

> Was it possible for Napoleon to win the battle? We answer in the negative. Why? On account of Wellington, on account of Blucher? No; on account of God. . . . Napoleon had been denounced in infinitude, and his fall was decided. He angered God.[8]

Aggressors do not inherit the earth; neither are they happy, in the end. It is the meek who inherit the earth. That's hard for us to believe because we're too nearsighted. America is only two hundred years old—a baby by historical standards. Her rise to grandeur has been relatively instantaneous. Her method for this meteoric ascension has been her aggressiveness.

But, when it comes to America's ability to endure as a civilization, the jury is still out, for the aggressive have never inherited the earth over the long haul. We had better start hearing what Jesus said about happy survival.

If it is the meek who survive happily, what does it mean to be meek? It does *not* mean to be cowardly, retreating, or broken in spirit. The Greek word translated *meek* had to do with the training of horses. A meek horse was one which maintained all of its innate courage, verve, and strength, but which allowed its powers to be directed toward productive ends.

Years ago, I read a story from Greek antiquity about a young soldier who was fighting in the Peloponnesian Wars. He wrote a letter to his sweetheart back home, telling her of a gift he was bringing her. It was a white stallion. "He is the most magnificent animal I've ever seen," said the soldier, "but he responds obediently to the slightest command . . . He allows his master to direct him to his full potential." And then he said, "He is truly a *meek* horse."

Darrel Royal, the football coach from the University of Texas, told me of a session he once had with his great Heisman Trophy winner, Earl Campbell. Earl had been dragging slowly back to the huddle after every play, causing unnecessary delays in the tempo of the game. Otherwise, he was a congenial, dedicated athlete who always gave one hundred percent.

Coach Royal didn't want to hurt the young freshman, whom he loved as a son, nor to take the edge off his dedication, but he did want to correct the one slight error. He began talking to Earl in general, obscure terms, hoping to approach the issue gently. Earl threw up his hands and said, "Wait a minute, Coach; I don't understand all this talk. Tell me straight. What is it you want me to do?" Royal paused a moment, then said, "When you're tackled, I want you to get up off your butt and run back to the huddle!"

"That I understand!" said Earl, "No problem. You're the coach, and you're my best friend . . . thanks for straightening me out." He was up and gone in a flash. The greatest collegiate running back in the world was a truly meek man.

The meek are those who subject themselves to discipline— that's the point. They are the teachable ones who realize that raw power is useless unless it is subjected to some "Coach" who knows how to develop it, nourish it, and bring it to its full potential.

Too often, we think of discipline as a negative term, that is, something you do to punish a person who has erred. It is a penalty. Really, discipline is positive. It's what you must do in order to get from where you are to where you want to be.

So Jesus is saying that happiness finds those who have set goals and have allowed all of their native energies to be channeled toward reaching those goals. The individuals and societies that survive happily are those that pay the price of discipline in order to get from where they are to where they want to be.

However, we must face the fact that there are many disciplined people who do not "survive happily." They set goals for themselves, accept "coaching," and achieve their goals, but they are not happy. What can be said about them? The same thing that was said earlier about those who mourn: *reaching goals won't make a person happy if he's reaching for the wrong goals!*

Happiness results when we're seeking the proper goal. And what is that? Again, it is the kingdom of

God—God's complete reign in our lives. Happiness never happens if our goals are the goals pressed upon us from the outside by culture, or if our goals are purely self-serving. That's why Jesus said, "He who would be greatest among you, let him be a servant."

Happiness Happens to the Yearners

Jesus' fourth saying about happiness reads: "Happy are those who hunger and thirst for the righteousness; they shall be filled" (Matt. 5:6). The image is that of a ravenous person who cannot be satisfied, no matter how much he eats.

Traditionally, this saying has been interpreted to mean that happiness comes to those who are never satisfied with their goodness—to those who constantly seek higher perfection and refuse to feel that they have "arrived." Happiness happens to those whose righteousness never satisfies them.

There's a lot to be said for the idea that a Christian must never be satisfied with his goodness, but I frankly think that reading this meaning into Jesus' words here is ridiculous!

Jesus is not talking about our righteousness; he's talking about God's. He's not saying, "Happy are those who hunger and thirst for right action on *their part.*" He's saying, "Happy are those who hunger and thirst for right action on *God's part.*"

"Righteousness" means "right action." It comes from a word meaning, "perpendicular," "straight." Happiness happens to those who cannot be satisfied until God makes this crooked world straight!

It's ridiculous to think that Jesus is telling us that happiness comes from a constant longing to be perfect, spotless saints. That's the stuff out of which legalistic, guilt-ridden religion is made. That's exactly what the Pharisees were teaching—that religion is a matter of confronting and conquering our faults, one by one.

No one is perfect in the sense of being faultless. I enjoy that story about the preacher who was trying to make this point by issuing his congregation a rhetorical challenge. "No one is perfect!" he boomed. "If anyone here this morning claims to be perfect, let him stand up, this minute." Whereupon a man promptly stood! The preacher was stunned. He hadn't expected this. "Do you mean to tell me, Sir, that you are claiming to be perfect?" he said. "No Sir," said the man, "I'm standing on behalf of my wife's first husband!"

The only one who is perfect is perhaps your wife's first husband or your husband's first wife. The rest of us don't qualify. Why then would Jesus be urging us to hunger and thirst for the unreachable? Remember my bias, stated earlier? The Sermon on the Mount is not a collection of ideals which we cannot reach; it's a collection of goals which we *can* reach. What we should be hungering and thirsting for is not our own perfect righteousness but that time when God will make the world straight, i.e. the kingdom of God.

We don't have to expend our energies in order to become worthy of the kingdom of God—we are already part of it by virtue of our acceptance of Jesus Christ. We have *already* entered the kingdom! Our task is not to concentrate upon every new sin that crops up in our lives, but to tell people of the goodness of God's kingdom, to tell them that they can enter the kingdom now, in spite of the fact that, like us, they do not deserve it.

Let's come at this business of "hungering and thirsting for righteousness" another way. If it means hungering and thirsting for personal perfection, there is no way we could ever be "filled" as Jesus promises. Have you ever tried to become perfect? If you have, you know that there's not an unhappier quest in the world. It's a never-ending struggle through guilt and heartbreak. You can't win for losing.

I was converted at the age of twenty, and my conversion was of the dramatic variety. I'm certain the local pastor rushed to the Monday pastor's conference to tell his colleagues of the "great victory." I was the last person in our town who would have been suspected as a candidate for conversion.

My newly found faith was simply indescribable. I saw things I never dreamed of. For six months I couldn't stop talking about it. My former friends ran when they saw me coming down the street. Word was out that I'd gone stark raving mad—a "holy-roller," a "fanatic."

The experience was so great that I decided to spend my life as a professional preacher. I went to school to learn and to prepare myself, and thus a sinister process began. For I was told immediately—in subtle and various ways—that in order to be an effective minister I had to achieve a certain standard of moral rectitude which I obviously hadn't yet reached. For instance, I was shown that I had some sins which I hadn't even known were sins! Smoking was one of them. Enjoying the beauty of a girl in a bathing suit was another. Dancing was another. Not being able to quote Scripture was another. There were many more.

I immediately set about trying to correct these "sins." But every time I conquered one, a new one emerged, and there I went again! It took me a long time, but I eventually began to see that the Good News which I had set out to proclaim had become Bad News. In hungering and thirsting for personal moral perfection, I had lost all of the creative ability and energy to love people and to introduce them to God's kingdom. In short, I had resorted to a treadmill of laws.

Remember that incident in which Jesus called a man to follow him, and the man said "OK, but first let me go and bury my father"? (Luke 9:57–62). Jesus said to him, "Let the dead bury their own dead; you go and preach the kingdom of God!" The Jewish law said that the man was obligated to see to his father's burial. It was the "righteous" thing to do. Why did Jesus give him such indecent orders, then?

I think Jesus was pointing to what we've been talking about here. As long as our focus of attention is on doing what the laws of personal perfection demand—as long as *that* is our chief hunger and thirst—we cannot give our full attention to telling the Good News of God's love and forgiveness.

So, happiness does not happen to those who are preoccupied with trying to be perfect. It happens to those who are preoccupied with working to bring about God's kingdom. It happens to those who are setting others free by telling them the Good News that God has entered our situation already and has forgiven us for our inability to be morally perfect. He has given us a new power to become what we were created to be, and he has made us his agents for ushering in the kingdom which is to come.

There are all sorts of hungers and thirsts—the hunger for food, for sex, for power, for self-esteem, for human love. And we've been sold the notion that happiness means filling our emotional and psychological and material bellies with these things. But we can never get enough, because they satisfy us only momentarily, and we have to go back for more. Therefore the happiness which they bring is also momentary. But Jesus says that permanent filling comes to those who hunger and thirst for God's action to bring his kingdom to reality. Happiness happens to those who long for the reign of God—in them and in the world—for *that will happen!*

Happiness Happens to the Merciful

At first glance, Jesus' next saying about how happiness happens doesn't unsettle us at all: "Happy are the merciful, for they shall receive mercy" (Matt. 5:7).

We should all agree that happiness comes from showing mercy to someone who is less fortunate than we are. Championing the underdog is America's favorite pastime. Anyone who has helped another of "lower station" knows the feeling of well-being which comes from being merciful.

But Jesus isn't limiting his command to underdogs alone. He's talking about the "overdogs" and the "equaldogs" too. He's talking about showing mercy to everyone, even those who do not fit our prescriptions for mercy!

That's where the X rating comes into this beatitude. For we would prefer to select our own recipients for mercy. In the first place, we would prefer to be merciful only if we can afford it. As someone has said, we would prefer to give away only the "sleeves of our vest"—that which cost us nothing. And then we would prefer to be merciful only if it can make us feel superior to the one who received our mercy.

Several years ago, I boarded a plane in Dallas enroute to Hawaii. Just as the plane was about to depart, a black man boarded and began searching for a seat. I didn't want to be crowded during the flight and secretly hoped he wouldn't choose the vacant seat next to me.

He tried to take a seat a couple of rows up, next to a

gentleman in a cowboy outfit. The cowboy said, "I don't want no colored folks next to me . . . move on!" He complied and moved to take the seat next to a woman directly across the aisle from the cowboy. The woman promptly placed her handbag in the seat before he could settle into it.

By this time, everyone on the plane was taking notice. I rose like a cavalier and said loudly, "Sir, I would count it an honor if you would join me"—emphasizing the "me" and glaring bravely at the cowboy and the woman.

"Forget it," said the black man. "I don't need no charity," and he went on down the aisle.

He had been abused enough in life to tell the difference between sincere mercy and that kind which is designed to give the mercy-giver a feeling of superiority. He was not rejecting my mercy because he was angry at all whites; he had read me like a book. He knew I was only trying to show what a grand, generous, and merciful fellow I was.

We prefer to select our own recipients, on our own terms, when it comes to being merciful. I've mentioned two of those terms; here's a third: We prefer to show mercy only to those who haven't hurt us, and can't hurt us if they are forgiven.

When I read of movie stars and other wealthy notables rushing to the defense of some convicted criminal, I cannot help but wonder whether they would do the same if they had been the criminal's victims. It's easy to show mercy to someone who has victimized someone else, especially if you can afford around-the-clock bodyguards and an elaborate security system at your mansion!

But as Jesus spoke of it, mercy isn't mercy unless it costs something; it isn't mercy unless it is given to one whom you regard as an equal; and it isn't mercy unless it is given to someone who has harmed you (and may still).

An example of true mercy comes out of the tragic assassination of Robert Kennedy at the hands of Sirhan Sirhan. Ethel Kennedy had paid a price—her husband's life. But she saw Sirhan Sirhan as a fellow human being with an equal right to life, and asked the presiding judge not to pronounce a death sentence.

From this we see that being merciful is not so romantic an exercise as we might think, for mercy is tied first of all to forgiveness, to canceling all of the debts we hold on those who have harmed us—the bad guys as well as the good.

To be merciful also means to give the other guy credit for being every bit as human as we are. I can't think of a better way to say it. Here's what I'm getting at: when someone does something which offends our sense of morality or something which directly harms us, we tend to immediately think of him as an "other." He becomes "the enemy" . . . an alien . . . a "they" . . . a subspecies . . . someone who is "not as we are."

When we begin to think this way, we can be led to do almost anything. It is a fact that in order to get a nation to wage war, one must convince its people that the enemy is not as *fully human* as they are. They must be taught to think of the enemy as "nips," "krauts," "gooks," "greasers," "wops," and the like. We cannot be merciless until we make this shift in our consciousness. We cannot kill our own flesh and blood; we can only kill "theys." A man who had killed his own son—a heroin addict—said, "He was no longer my son. He was an animal; he had no personality."

To be merciful requires that we give the other guy credit for being every bit as human as we are. From my youth, I was taught that black people were not "our kind." They had no loyalty to family; they rarely married legally; they would steal if given the chance; they were inherently less intelligent than whites.

Then, when I was sixteen, I had occasion to live with a black family for several weeks. To my utter surprise, they were concerned about the same things as my family—their son's grades, whether he brushed his teeth, who his friends were, how to meet mortgage payments, how to pay a tithe to their church.

After a few days, I wasn't even aware of the difference in our skin pigmentation. I was no longer living with a black family; I was living with George, Bess, and Henry Payne! Needless to say, it was an experience which led me to ask some serious questions about our society's interpretation of mercy.

Giving the other guy credit for being as human as we are was the key factor behind Jesus' mercifulness. At the Cross he said, "Father forgive them; for they know not what they do" (Luke 23:34, KJV). I don't think he was referring primarily to their ignorance in that statement; he wasn't saying, "Father, forgive them, for they don't know that they are killing the Messiah." I think he was pointing to the fact that he understood what was driving them. They were threatened people, driven by panic and fear. And when people are driven to panic, they do things which are out of character. In a word, Jesus was giving them credit for acting like humans.

Recognizing the essential humanness of others also accounts for his association with the so-called "sinners" of his day. It was his mercy toward them which got him into hot water with the religious establishment. Instead of speaking harsh words to the "sinners," Jesus spoke harshly only to the Pharisees! And his quarrel with the religionists centered in the fact that they refused to acknowledge that the sinners were as human as they! Of course, the result of their refusal was the absence of mercy.

Happiness happens to the merciful. How so? What does being merciful have to do with making us happy? Well, for one thing, the opposite of mercy is hating, and hating is hard work. It takes a lot out of a person. It eats up his creativity. It gives him time to do little else except feed his hatred.

Take Melville's classic story, *Moby Dick,* as an example. Captain Ahab hates the great whale, Moby Dick, who has crippled him. He's obsessed with killing the whale no matter what. Every waking hour, Ahab is consumed with tracking him down. He devises elaborate rituals which are designed to infect his crew with a similar passion for vengeance.

As the plot unfolds, it becomes obvious that Ahab, not Moby Dick, is the real victim. Ahab is the one who is imprisoned, hunted, and driven by hatred, by the complete inability to love anything. In the end, he kills everything around him—the whale, the crew, and himself.

Hating is hard work. It saps all that is potentially good and creative. Happiness happens only to those who can create and grow, and we cannot create and grow until we practice mercy.

Now, listen to the rest of what Jesus says about the merciful: "They shall receive mercy." There are no hidden meanings here; the message is plain: you get what you give. If you give mercilessness, you get mercilessness. If you give mercy, you get mercy. From whom? From God!

Is this too simplistic? Not at all. Look at the parable Jesus told about the wicked debtor (Matt. 18:23–35). A master was checking up on his accounts when he discovered that one of his servants owed him millions. When he demanded payment, the servant pled for mercy. The master forgave him and let him go. Then the man went out, met a fellow servant who owed him only a few dollars, and demanded payment. The fellow servant also pled for mercy, but the wicked servant had him thrown into prison until he could pay.

When the master heard of it, he hauled the wicked servant before him. "You worthless slave!" he said, "I forgave you the whole amount, just because you asked me to. You should have had mercy on your fellow servant, just as I had mercy on you." The master had the wicked servant thrown into jail until he could pay back the entire sum he owed.

And Jesus concluded, "That is how my Father will treat you, if you do not show mercy to your brother."

There are no loopholes here. The merciful receive mercy; the unmerciful do not. We get what we give. It's nonsense to believe that because I'm a born-again Christian I am exempt from showing mercy.

And yet we know that, if this is true, everyone of us stands condemned, for everyone of us refuses at one time or another to show mercy. That's why Jesus' words make us so nervous!

But there they are! Happiness happens to the merciful, because the merciful receive mercy. It is not God's love which is at stake here; it is our happiness. If we are unmerciful we shall be unhappy. If we are merciful, happiness will find us.

Happiness Happens to the Single-minded

Jesus' next saying about happiness is that it happens to the "pure in heart." "Happy are the pure in heart; they shall see God" (Matt. 5:8).

Obviously, he doesn't mean "happy are the spotless." There is a "stain" on the heart of everyone. Nor was he talking about so-called "pure motives," as some would have us believe. He was not saying, "Happy are those who have good intentions in everything they do." There is no such thing as a pure motive. We are too broken, too bent on looking out for old "Number One" to have pure motives.

Recently, in our city, a schoolteacher was murdered by one of his students in front of the entire class. Our community went into a shock reaction. The lack of discipline in the schools was decried; recriminations were hurled back and forth. Several of us began to search for a way in which the community could respond, rather than merely react, to this tragedy. A committee was formed to raise a trust fund for the infant son of the teacher. The news media and representatives from every segment of the community united. I was elected chairman of the effort, and as a result appeared on TV and in the newspapers almost daily for several weeks.

During the drive, I was having lunch in a restaurant when a colleague approached my table. After initial conversation he said, "The main reason you're involved in this is to get free publicity for yourself and your church. You're always looking for a way to get your name in print!"

I didn't take the trouble to inform him that the reason he felt obliged to dress me down was that he would have enjoyed the publicity *himself!* The fact was that there was a lot of truth to what he said. I would hope that my motives were higher than my own self-aggrandizement—that they were aimed at helping that child and drawing the community together—but I can't deny that I had thought of the benefits to be reaped for myself as well. At least *one* of my motives for accepting the leadership of the drive had been the good it would do for me and for the church's image.

There's no such thing as a pure motive, if it means complete selflessness. So I don't think Jesus is telling us that happiness happens only to the "pure in motive."

I think he is referring to the *simplification of life*. He says, "Happy are those who refuse to complexify their lives, those with singular allegiances to the kingdom of God." Thoreau once said, "In proportion as I have simplified my existence, I have found the universe to be friendly; in proportion as I have complexified my existence, I have found the universe to be hostile. . . . Simplify! Simplify! Simplify!"[9] Kierkegaard said it another way: "Purity of heart is to will one thing."[10]

The happy people of this world are those who know the merit of having no more than one God, one passion, one overarching goal in life. Isn't this the real message behind the story of Adam and Eve's "fall by fruit"? God has given them the entire garden to rule over, except for one tree. And that tree stands as the constant reminder that he is their God and they are his servants. The garden is not to be their God; he who created the garden and gave them dominion over it is to be their God.

They are in a state of perfect bliss so long as they keep this order in mind. But the moment they eat of the tree, and thereby substitute love of the garden for their love of God, life begins to turn sour. They discover, for one thing, that they now have a sex drive which they can't control, so they have to start wearing clothes. Work is no longer a creative fulfillment; it is now sweat and toil and a curse. Many of the animals they once named and lived in harmony with are now threats to their existence. And of course, the battle of

the sexes has also begun. Male now dominates female.
They are no longer complements to each other's existence, but threats to each other. Childbearing is no
longer a joyful participation with God in creation; it too
is a painful, anxiety-filled chore.

In short, when Adam and Eve try to take on more
than one God, they lose both God and the garden! And
they also lose happiness. They no longer are running
life; it is running them.

"Happy are those who simplify their existence"—we
don't believe that! It's an X-rated idea in this society
which believes it can have both God and "the garden."
Our society believes that happiness comes only to the
"versatile in heart," i.e. to those who have multiple goals
and fill every living moment with frenzied activity.

Witness how concerned we are to project the image
of being "busy persons." We go to ridiculous lengths to
conceal our desires for leisure. If we're idle for a
moment, we think we're committing a sin against the
Goddess of Busy. We Americans worship *doing*. If a
person isn't busy *doing*, he's thought to be worthless,
nonproductive. Persons are not valued by what they
are, but by what they can do. The more project and the
more productivity, the more worthy the person.

I once pastored in a prosperous farming community
which thrived on the philosophy, "happy are the
versatile in heart." Almost everyone had at least two
jobs and three civic and religious causes. The unpar-
donable sin was to sleep late into the morning. Since I
had always been a late sleeper, I was in trouble from the
beginning.

I endeavored to reform and started rising at six, after
which I did the only thing there was to do in a rural
town at six A.M.—I joined all the rest of the early risers
at the Caison House Coffee Shop. They were a super

bunch of guys—God never created any better. I don't wish to belittle them in the least. For the most part they gathered each morning for the fellowship and the camaraderie. But I discovered that they gathered *so early* for another reason. It was the only way they could feel justified in enjoying a pure and simple bull session which had nothing to do with productivity! To have gathered at 10 A.M. would have been considered a mark of idleness.

Often, I hear urban businessmen reflecting the same mentality. If they take a day off to be with the children or to go fishing, they do it only because they are "drained from overwork." It's as though we feel that we do not deserve relaxation unless it qualifies as *recuperation!*

Even those who are rebelling against this maddening demand that we be "versatile in heart" present interesting contradictions. Most of the meditators and self-analysts I know practice their art according to a demanding schedule! Meditation becomes an imperative, an "ought"! It's, "Up at dawn and hip, hip to meditation! Gotta stay with the program!"

Is it any wonder that a society which so regiments itself toward doing homage to so many gods is so unhappy?

Happiness happens to those who set their hearts on one program: bringing in the kingdom. Why does happiness find them? It finds them because they alone see God, that is, his presence in the now and his reign over the future.

The so-called "seers" of history have always been those who simplified their existence. Moses couldn't see God until he left the hubbub of Pharoah's court and went to the backside of the desert. Elijah didn't hear God in the wind and the fire and the storm of "busyness," but in a still, small voice at the mouth of a cave. Paul was touched on the road to Damascus, but he received his vocation during his three years in the desert.

Maybe we cannot flee to the backside of the desert, or to Elijah's cave, but we can refine our allegiances and pare down our priorities. For happiness finds those who purify their commitments—they see God.

Happiness Happens to the Peacemakers

Jesus' seventh bit of advice is that happiness happens to peacemakers: "They shall be called the sons of God" (Matt. 5:9). As was the case with his statement on being merciful, we could hardly call this an X-rated idea at first glance. After all, everyone knows that solving disputes and reconciling differences makes people happy.

Nevertheless, I say this idea would be unnerving to our society, if its real meaning were understood. For most of us regard peace as a kind of nonaggressive coexistence in which two sides "leave each other in peace."

A friend who is a judge told me a story which illustrates the popular notion of peace. He was trying a habitual offender whom he had known most of his life. The fellow had prior convictions for larceny and manslaughter, and was now convicted for rape and attempted murder. Before pronouncing sentence, the judge said, "Jim, I've known you since we were children, and you have never lived six months of your adult life without committing a crime. I want to ask you a personal question. Does your religious conscience ever bother you? Have you ever thought of what God thinks of your actions?"

"Sure," said Jim, "I've always been at peace with God. . . . He don't bother me, and I don't bother him!"

The common belief is that peace between two parties means not bothering each other—you live your life, and I'll live mine. Peace means *detente,* to use a political concept which was popular in recent days. It's a nonaggression pact.

Jesus has a different idea in mind when he speaks of peace. To him, peace means reconciliation. People were at peace with each other when they worked together, cared for each other, helped each other. In a word, they were at peace when they were in a *community of mutual dependence,* not when they marked off separate territories and refrained from encroachment. People were at peace when they said "We," not when they said "I" and "You."

This means that peacemakers are those who bring people together as one family, not those who merely negotiate cease-fires. And, as I see it, many do not view the peacemaking role as one which results in happiness. They had much rather fan the ashes of ancient rivalries than promote togetherness. They would prefer to appeal to longstanding prejudices and injustices— which practice, I might add, seems to be the stock and trade of some politicians and leaders of social reform these days.

In other words, we don't seem to believe that bringing people together as one community is a happiness-producing exercise. Witness the fact that most of our heroes are not peacemakers but *victors*—the strong macho-types who conquer the enemy. Happiness comes to him who vanquishes the opposition, not to him who makes the opposition his friend.

I saw a movie years ago which points up how we really feel about peacemaking. It was one of those science-fiction horror films entitled *The Thing.* The scene was set in an arctic wasteland where a group of military scientists and soldiers were encamped. They encountered a horrible superhuman monster who threatened to devour them. One of the scientists wanted to attempt to communicate with the monster, to befriend it and study it. But the rest of the company, led by the hero of the movie, wanted to destroy the creature.

As the plot unfolded, the scientist was caricatured as a coward and a fool. Eventually, because of his foolhardiness, he became one of the victims of the Thing. The hero, however, killed the monster, after which he and a shapely technician lived happily ever after.

The message: happiness comes to those who destroy the enemy; unhappiness is the lot of them who are naive enough to believe in making the enemy a friend.

Another way to express the modern notion of peacemaking is to say that it is a matter of conceding to others only that which will guarantee our security. This is America's peace policy. It is the negative approach. It does not seek to establish an international community, but rather to keep the enemy at bay. And it candidly refers to itself as "maintaining the balance of terror." Imagine that—we believe that peace can be had through terror! That may seem sensible, when we consider that there has been no worldwide confrontation since the invention of nuclear terror-weapons, but it is absurd to believe that mutual fear can ever bring world peace.

Yet we seem committed to pursue peace on this basis, and not only on the international level. Married couples often attempt to build their relationships on this concept of peace. They maintain a truce, not a communal relationship. In these relationships, peace means the peaceful coexistence of two separate entities. Each makes concessions only to the extent that the marriage is secured. Even premarital legal contracts are gaining popularity. I know a couple who executed a duly notarized contract which stated such minutae as who would take out the garbage and whose parents would be visited at Christmas—all of this done in the belief that a peaceful marriage could be guaranteed by a proper, legal, truce arrangement!

As I said earlier, Jesus' idea of peace is reconciliation, and peacemakers are the agents of reconciliation. But there is another factor which underlies these concepts—namely, that all reconciliation between persons stems from reconciliation with God. We cannot become a community until we are reconciled with God. You and I cannot be at peace with each other until we are at peace with him who made us.

Therefore, the peacemakers are they who are at work reconciling people to God. Trying to effect reconciliation between people by leaving God out of the process inevitably leads to frustration. A good example of this fact is the so-called "Peace Movement" of the late sixties and early seventies. Youth were running to and fro flashing the peace sign, wearing peace T-shirts, and destroying the combative symbols of American patriotism. At the same time, they were calling policemen "pigs," and saying "You can't trust anyone over thirty."

They were effective in stopping the Viet Nam War, but not in producing the kind of peace which men like Charles Reich predicted they would produce. The "new consciousness" Reich predicted in his *The Greening of America* has not arrived. Why? Because there can be no peace until peace is found in God. We can't love our brothers and sisters until we love our Father.

All of this is to say that happiness happens to the peacemaker *only if he is trying to make the right kind of peace—peace between God and man.* Happiness does not happen to the peace-hopers or to the peace-eulogizers who promote nonaggression and attempt to maintain the balance of terror. It happens to those who introduce others to him who is the Prince of Peace. They are the sons of God.

Happiness Happens to the Persecuted

We don't have much trouble recognizing that the eighth beatitude is unnerving, for Jesus says, "Happiness happens to those who are persecuted for trying to do what is right" (Matt. 5:10). From our viewpoint the unhappiest experience of all is to be punished because we are doing right. How could anyone enjoy being persecuted for doing the right thing? It sounds like masochism, like Jesus is urging us to seek martyrdom.

How can we make sense of this apparent absurdity? First consider this: it is a fact of life that sooner or later every human being will be "persecuted," that is, he will have to suffer. Suffering is inevitable, no matter who or what we are.

So the key question is: what are we going to suffer *for?* Will it be for something which cannot lead to happiness or for something which *will* lead to happiness?

Jesus is saying that happiness happens to those who suffer for the right reason. It's the same idea we spoke of earlier in our discussion of the beatitude on mourning. Since we're going to suffer anyway, let our suffering be for that which can lead to happiness. And what is that? Again I answer, it is the kingdom of God.

Persecution which comes from our attempts to establish the kingdom is the kind of persecution which leads to happiness, *because our attempts cannot be in vain.* We know that the kingdom will come, because it has already come. Therefore, we know that no effort is wasted when God is keeping score.

This point has a special meaning to me at this precise moment. Each year I take a month away from my usual duties to write as I am doing now. I rent a condominium by the sea, so that my wife and children can recreate while I work at a nearby cabin which is owned by my parents. During the month, my brother, sister, and parents bring their families down on the weekends. Therefore, I enjoy the dual benefit of working and reuniting with the Mann clan.

However, this summer the experience has been painful for me. Everyone in the family except myself is highly successful in the business world. They hunt, fish, and travel all over the globe. They are immersed in the world of limousines, furs, yachts, private airplanes, and all of the exotic experiences that go with those possessions.

I love my family. They are sensitive, hard-driving, honest folk, and if I ever needed anything they could give they would respond without hesitation. But the blatant truth is that I do not fit into their world. We have very little in common save our bloodlines. I'm writing this on Saturday, a day I usually take off from writing, but this morning I had an experience which motivated me to pick up the pen.

To put it simply, I am feeling "persecuted." I am hurt. My sense of self-worth is threatened. Today I sat at coffee with the men of the family and listened to their excitement over an upcoming hunting trip to Alaska which I shall never make. I heard them recount a recent trip to the South Pacific which cost more money than I make in two years working eighty hours a week. Outside, my '73 Chevy with eighty thousand miles on it was parked between three eighteen-thousand-dollar Cadillacs. My brother-in-law, wanting to include me in the group, asked me where I was going to hunt deer this fall, and I had to make up a cock-and-bull story about how I had lost interest in hunting. The truth is, I can't afford it!

I politely excused myself and drove my old Chevy back to the study where I'm now writing this. I had a deep sense of bitterness. I picked up this manuscript on which I've been working twelve hours a day, and for which I'll be lucky if I receive enough income to pay the month's rent on the condominium.

"It's not fair!" I said to God. "While they sit draped in the lap of luxury, I am scratching with every ounce of my being to create something most people won't read anyway!"

I began to read over what I have written, and lo and behold it began to speak *to me!* No effort for the kingdom of God is wasted, because it is God who is keeping score! Everyone is persecuted in one way or another; happiness happens to those who are persecuted for doing what God wants!

Don't misread me. I'm not saying my family is doing the wrong thing; I'm saying that if I chose to pursue their lifestyles, it would be the wrong pursuit *for me.* Happiness would not happen, because their pursuits are not the pursuits which God has ordained for me.

I'm also saying that, regardless of whether this book enjoys a wide readership, it has already served to straighten out its author, who suffered a momentary siege of feeling sorry for himself and of questioning his worth as a human being.

I recognize that this maudlin account violates the canons of etiquette for writers. One simply doesn't focus upon such self-serving subjects. I also realize that my hurt may sound silly. There are many of you who have it worse than I. But regardless of how shallow the hurts of others may seem, they are real hurts to those who are hurting.

Anyway, I hope you will overlook my sentimentality enough to hear the message: Happiness happens to those who suffer for their efforts in the kingdom. Nietzsche said that a man can endure any 'how' if he has a 'why.' We can endure and transform any suffering, if beyond that suffering we have a purpose, an ultimate concern.

Obviously, the world's concept of happiness is a persecution-free existence. All that was said earlier about America's idolatrous pursuit of happiness applies here. We have sold our souls to the evasion of all unpleasantness. The aim of most of our technological genius is to alleviate the necessity of having to toil and deal with the "hard things" of life. We seem to have forgotten that it is only through fire that the human spirit is refined into gold. Take away suffering, and we take away that which makes us essentially humans who were created in the image of God.

Summary

We have tried to show that Jesus's ideas about happiness as expressed in the Beatitudes have a way of making us nervous. They appear to be idealistic, if not absurd. And they seem absurd because the world does not understand that happiness is a result instead of a goal. We do not go out and find happiness; it finds us while we are pursuing something else—the kingdom of God.

Once we understand this, the question is, how do we pursue the kingdom of God in such a way that happiness finds us? The answer is contained in the eight Beatitudes which introduce the Sermon on the Mount.

First, happiness happens to the "poor in spirit." To be poor in spirit means to accept our humanness, our dependence upon God for life and being. But this idea is unnerving to a world which is bent on denying human dependence. The world's motto is, "Happy are the inflated in spirit." And the world is unhappy.

Second, "Happiness happens to those who mourn," says Jesus, "to those who cry for the same things that make God cry"—namely, the things which impede the kingdom's progress. In other words, happiness happens to those who mourn over the obstructions to the kingdom, for it is only this kind of grieving which will ultimately find comfort.

Third, happiness comes to those who submit their innate powers to God's discipline, i.e. to the "meek." Meek means coachable. The world says that happiness comes to those who dominate and conquer. Jesus says happiness comes to those who accept discipline. They shall inherit the "earth"—the earth which God will one day re-create.

Fourth, happiness happens to those who "hunger and thirst for righteousness"—not for personal perfection, but for the action of God to make the world "right." Our pursuit of personal perfection is doomed to frustration; it is an ideal which is unreachable. Our happiness does not rest on what we can do, but on what God is *going* to do. Therefore, we are to preoccupy ourselves not with our personal perfection, but with helping God establish his kingdom.

The fifth piece of advice about happiness is that it happens to the merciful. Mercy means mercy to all—those who we think do not qualify for our mercy as well as those who we think deserve it. To be merciful means to give the other guy credit for being every bit as worthy of God's grace as we are. The world says happiness comes from being "discriminately merciful." Jesus says happiness comes from being "indiscriminately" merciful.

Happiness also happens to the "pure in heart"—that is, to those who simplify their priorities and "will one thing." The world says happiness comes only to those who are "versatile in heart"—to those who complicate their lives by serving many gods with many projects.

In the seventh place, Jesus says happiness happens to the "peacemakers." A peacemaker is one who reconciles persons with persons by reconciling them to God. The world sees making peace as a matter of effecting nonaggressive coexistence between separate peoples; peace means, "You don't bother me, and I won't bother you." Jesus views peace as united interdependence, in which people become responsible for and to each other.

Finally, happiness happens to those who are persecuted for trying to bring in the kingdom. Everyone must suffer for something; happiness comes to those who suffer for the right cause—the kingdom of God. The world says happiness comes to those who evade suffering; Jesus says happiness comes to those who choose their reason for suffering.

No doubt it is evident that in this chapter I have refrained from saying what happiness is. I have done it on purpose, for happiness is that indefinable something for which we all yearn but cannot put into words. If we were to find it, we would recognize it, but we can't define it. We know what it's *not*, all right, but we cannot say what it is. Whatever it is, Jesus says it will find us when we dare to begin pursuing the kingdom of God. It will find us, *partially*, now. It will find us, *fully*, in the age to come.

QUESTIONS FOR STUDY

1. How does Jesus's view of happiness differ from the most widely held view in modern society?
2. How would you explain the phrase, "Happiness is a result"?
3. What is idolatry, and how does it relate to happiness?
4. What are the Beatitudes, and where are they found?
5. What does it mean:
   —to be poor in spirit?
   —to mourn?
   —to be meek?
   —to hunger and thirst for rightness?
   —to be merciful?
   —to be pure in heart?
   —to be a peacemaker?
   —to be persecuted for righteousness' sake?
6. How do the above relate to happiness?

CHAPTER TWO

UNNERVING NOTIONS ABOUT CHRISTIAN STRATEGY

(Matthew 5:13–48)

What's a Nice God Like You . . .

Late one evening some years ago, I was sitting in a hotel coffeeshop which was located adjacent to a bar. From where I sat, I had a full view of the combo, the dance floor, and most of the patrons. The topless waitresses were meandering through the crowd of assorted drunks and riotous merrymakers. The din was deafening even in the coffee shop; I could imagine what it was like inside the bar.

The bandleader announced that it was time for the group to take a break, and thanked the people for their attention. Hardly anyone was paying attention; they were either too preoccupied or benumbed to care.

Then the leader said, "Wait a minute . . . I have something to say." Still there was no recognition. "Since this is the Christmas season," he continued, "I would like to tell you about an amazing experience I've recently enjoyed." The crowd grew quieter. "Two months ago, I met Jesus Christ face to face." The room was silent now. "I always believed in God, but now he is real to me. I never knew that life could be so good!"

For the next five minutes, the young man shared his Christian experience to a rapt audience. Topless barmaids and drunks alike didn't miss a word. When he finished, they gave him a standing ovation!

I was shocked! I kept saying, "What's a nice God, like mine, doing in a place like this! If the guy were *really* a Christian, he wouldn't be playing the Beatles in a bar; he'd be playing 'The Old Rugged Cross' in a church!" The very idea of soiling the name of Jesus in a den of booze and bongos and bare flesh was more than I could take. And if that weren't enough, the bleary-eyed beasts had had the audacity to applaud!

I was twenty-six years old then, and like many religious zealots I was of the dogmatic opinion that the world was divided into the two realms of "sacred and secular." In fact, that very night I had given an impassioned exposé of the "sin of dancing" to a group of teenagers at a local church. I had used as my chief argument the age-old question, "If Jesus came back tonight, would you want him to find you on the dance floor?"

Little did I understand in those days the implications of what I was saying and feeling regarding how a Christian is to relate to the present world. It didn't occur to me that I was advocating that Christians withdraw into a sacred cocoon. I didn't know that my Christian strategy was that of an Indian raiding party which dashes out into enemy territory, gathers a few scalps for Jesus, and then dashes back to the sacred stronghold called the church.

In short, I didn't recognize that I was the victim of one of the great religious heresies of history. It is the heresy of sanctimonious exclusivism. It was popular in Jesus' day, and it still is. His strategy for changing the world—for bringing in the kingdom—is just as unnerving today as it ever was.

The religious people of his day believed, as we do, that God's kingdom was coming. The "day of the Lord" would dawn inevitably, because the world belonged to God. Their quarrel with Jesus, however, arose over the question of what God's people were to do in the interim, that is, until the kingdom came? How were God's people to relate to the unbelieving society? What was the believer's posture?

The Jewish answer was twofold. First, God's people were to remain as a separate entity, untainted by association with unbelievers. If the sinners wanted to come to them, so be it, but they would not mix with the sinners.

Second, God's people were to live by a legal code while awaiting the kingdom. The goal of every believer was to remain "legally righteous" until the day of the Lord. Keeping the laws of Moses and the Prophets was the fare one must pay to enter the kingdom.

In other words, the Jewish strategy for relating to the world was "withdraw and keep the Law!"

But Jesus proposed a different strategy, and it got him into trouble. His contemporaries couldn't tolerate it, because to do so would have required that they revolutionize their entire way of thinking and doing. I dare say it would do the same to us.

Jesus' ideas about how the Christian is to relate to his society are contained in that portion of the Sermon on the Mount which we call Matthew 5:13–48. In essence, he says that the Christian's task is "to preserve" and "to point." These two ideas can best be explained by looking at the text itself.

Salt and Light: Preserve and Point

First, Jesus says that Christians are to be like salt and like light (Matt. 5:13–14). Salt was primarily used as a preservative in those days; it was the only available means of checking the processes of decay in foods. So this passage implies that the Christian should be a preserver. A preserver of what? From what Jesus says later, I think he meant a preserver of the world's order, a check against chaos and disintegration. But up to now, he simply says a Christian is to preserve. If he does not, he is like salt which has lost its preserving power; it is good for nothing save being thrown out on the ground.

Second, the Christian is to be like light. What kind of light? The kind of light which shows people things they cannot see otherwise—the light which points them toward God and causes them to glorify him.

So the Christian is to be a preserver and a pointer. He preserves the world's order against the forces of decadence, and he serves as a light which points men to God. I like the analogy of a channel beacon which points the ships toward the harbor. A Christian is to be a beacon which points the way to God. The Christian doesn't point to himself; he points beyond himself.

But the question arises as to how the Christian is to go about preserving the world order (salt) and pointing the world toward God (light). Jesus proceeds to answer this question by comparing his commandments to the commandments of the Jewish law (Matt. 5:17–20).

Being Legal Is Necessary

He has not come to abolish laws of Moses, he says, but to "fill them up"—to complete them, to give them ultimate meaning. Anyone who does not obey the laws is not fit for the kingdom of God.

What does this have to do with the Christian's role as preserver? It means that he must preserve by obeying laws. A Christian is not exempted from keeping the rules because he is a Christian. The world cannot survive without order, and order demands law.

In a word, the Christian preserves the world order against decay by keeping the laws of the land. If the laws are unjust, he may break them, but that doesn't mean he is freed from paying the consequences of breaking them.

During the Viet Nam war, a Christian friend of mine deliberately refused to be inducted into military service.

He applied for a conscientious objector's status, and was turned down because he said that he was not opposed to war in general, but to that *particular* war.

He was intending to flee to Canada, and wanted to know whether I thought his intentions were "Christian." I replied that I was in total sympathy with his view of the injustice of the war, and also with his refusal to be inducted, but that I could not agree with his intentions to escape punishment for his actions. For whereas the Bible teaches that it is right to defy an unjust law, it also teaches that laws are necessary for the preservation of order. Therefore, the only alternative the Christian has is to suffer the consequences of his defiance in the hope that his punishment will awaken the government to the law's injustice.

The Christian is a preserver, and preservation means obedience to the law. A lawless Christian is as useless as salt without saltiness.

Being Legal Is Not Enough

But now Jesus presses a harder demand. He says, "Except your righteousness exceeds that of the Pharisees and the lawyers, you cannot enter the kingdom of God." The Christian is not only a preserver who obeys the law, he is also a pointer who does more than the law requires! To be light means to point the world to something higher—the kingdom of God. And to do that means to exceed what the law requires!

For the Jews, doing right from the legal point of view was all that was required. Unfortunately, that idea is also held in our present society. Give credit again to Alexander Solzhenitsyn for being the most recent to point out the deadly effects of this mentality upon the Western world. He says that our society is conveniently based on the letter of the law. No one is urged to restrain himself beyond what the law requires. If one is legally right, nothing else matters.

Therefore, everyone operates at the extreme limit of the legal frame. An oil company is legally blameless when it purchases a new type of energy in order to prevent its use. A food manufacturer can poison his product to make it last longer, and is respectable because he is legal. After all, people are free not to buy it.

"I have spent all my life under a Communist regime," says Solzhenitsyn, "and I will tell you that a society without any objective legal scale is a terrible one indeed. But a society with no other scale but the legal one is not quite worthy of man either. . . . The letter of the law is too cold and formal to have a beneficial influence on society. Whenever the tissue of life is woven of legalistic relations, there is an atmosphere of moral mediocrity, paralyzing man's noblest impulses."[1]

Solzhenitsyn does not see the American way of life as an alternative to the oppressive philosophy of his native country. The American system, based upon materialism and legality, is as destructive of the human spirit as Communism or Naziism. He calls for a society which goes beyond what is required by law, a society which uses existing laws to point itself forward to a higher form of human existence. Jesus of Nazareth said the same thing two thousand years ago in the Sermon on the Mount! "Unless your righteousness exceeds that of the legalists, you shall not enter the kingdom of God."

How is a Christian to relate to his society? Thus far, we have answered that he is to preserve it by penetrating it and permeating it, like salt permeates and preserves food from decay. In practical terms, this means that the Christian is to obey the law. But he must also go beyond the legal so that he is like a channel beacon pointing the society toward God.

Salt and Light and Murder

Stating the above truths is not enough. We need some examples. In a sense, the rest of the Sermon on the Mount contains examples of what it means to be salt and light—preservers and pointers. However, in this chapter, we shall look at only five of the examples Jesus gives. For, as I said in the introduction, the Sermon is difficult to outline symmetrically.

Thus, what are some examples of the salt (preserver) and light (pointer) strategy which the Christian is to use in relating to his world? The first example Jesus gives has to do with murder (Matt. 5:21–26).

The law of the land prohibited murder. Everyone would agree with the sanity of that law, in any society. There can be no order in a culture which allows for indiscriminate killing. And Jesus supports that law totally: "All they that take the sword shall perish with the sword," he said elsewhere (Matt. 26:52, KJV). So, obviously, the Christian is to observe the law in this respect. By so doing, he is performing his salt-function, that is, preserving society's order.

But in order to be "more than legal"—in order to be a pointer (a light) for his society—*the Christian must refrain from even being angry at his neighbor!*

The Jewish law didn't deal with the subjects of anger and hatred which are the seeds of murder. A person could hate all he wanted to, so long as he didn't commit the overt act of homicide. Refraining from the overt act is not enough for the Christian, says Jesus. If he wants to be a pointer/light for his society, he must not only refrain from commiting homicide; he must also refrain from hating.

Jesus fills out his point about anger with three additional illustrations: (1) If one Jew pronounced a verbal curse upon another Jew, he was required to

stand before the council of Justice (the Sanhedrin).
Jesus says that if a Christian calls *anyone*, Jew or non-
Jew, even a mild name like "fool," he will stand before
the Council of Hell! (2) If a Jew were at odds with his
neighbor, he could go to the Temple and worship
without qualms. Feuds had nothing to do with worship.
Jesus says a feud with a neighbor must be settled before
one can worship. Otherwise, worship is an insult to
God. (3) The common way of settling disputes in Jesus'
day was to let a court decide. Jesus says to settle disputes
before they get to court!

It should be obvious why I have contended
throughout this book that Jesus' ideas in the Sermon
make us nervous. Has our society heard him? Is this the
way we Christians relate to the world today? No! Like
our Jewish ancestors, we are content to settle for that
which is merely legal.

For example, anger runs rampant within the Christian community. Name-calling is the order of the day.
In my denomination, it seems to be the favorite sport
among ministers; we seem to be label-crazy. Someone
has said that our preachers are like warships cruising
the coastline of a world which has shut them out.
Instead of landing and infiltrating, the ships are content to fire occasional salvos ashore. But mostly, they
fire at each other! I've often thought that we ministers
could at least adopt the professional ethics of physicians
and attorneys and declare a moratorium on publicly
attacking one another.

Furthermore, think of the anger that flourishes
among the members of almost every local congregation.
On any given Sunday, *Christians* who are at odds with
each other can be found at worship. Have we really
heard what Jesus said, that it's useless to worship God
when we're at odds with a neighbor?

And think about the courts. I dare say the dockets would be drastically reduced if Christians resolved their differences according to Jesus' prescription.

In Jesus' day, interpersonal relationships were based upon the principle of reciprocity. One should be decent only to those who were decent to him. If they were indecent to you, you have every cause to be indecent to them; the code was tit for tat, an eye for an eye, response in kind. Jesus taught "response in contrast." Be decent, he said, whether others are decent or not. *In other words, don't let your rightness depend upon another's conduct.*

Isn't that what's killing our current society? Too many of us let what the other guy does determine what we do.

In January of 1977, capital punishment was revived in this country. One Gary Gilmore was executed at his own request. Polls revealed that most Americans agreed with his execution. This is no place to debate the pros and cons of capital punishment, but I do think one thing needs to be said—namely that Gary Gilmore succeeded in getting our society to allow his conduct to determine our conduct. Gilmore was a vicious and cold-blooded killer. Guilt loves company. When society would not "accompany" him by copying his act of killing, he set about forcing us to. He made us kill because he killed.

The illustration may have holes in it; for instance, I recognize that there is a difference between killing and murder. But the fact remains that we allowed his taking of a life to motivate us to take a life. And Jesus' principle still applies: the Christian must go beyond what is legally required. The law says don't murder; Jesus says, don't hate. And *that* notion makes this present world very nervous.

Salt and Light and Adultery

The second example of how a Christian is to relate to his world deals with the subject of adultery (Matt. 5:27–30). Adultery was forbidden in the Jewish society for the same obvious reasons as murder. Adultery creates chaos. It destroys the foundations of community. We all know that . . . wait a minute, *we all should know it!* But apparently we don't.

The Bible places adultery alongside murder when it comes to the actions which most certainly break down a civilization. However, American society seems to have forgotten this. Extramarital affairs are both commonplace and "winked-at" nowadays. They enhance an actor's climb to popularity and are no longer considered a detriment to a politician's career.

Historian J. D. Unwin studied eighteen civilizations in an effort to determine which factors best accounted for their disintegration.[2] He reached an interesting conclusion concerning a society's sexual mentality. He says that at some point every civilization, in order to survive, must choose between sexual promiscuity or restraint. If it chooses the former, its power of creativity, productivity, and discipline are lost. The decline of each civilization he studied was accompanied by a sexual "heating up." His conclusion was that every society has one of two choices: either sexual promiscuity and decline, or sexual restraint and growth.

With that aside, let's get back to our main subject. Christians are to refrain from adultery. This is their salt-function, their means of preserving the order of society. They are not exempted from the law because they are Christians.

But here again, Jesus expands the commandment to include the Christian's light-function. The Christian is required to go beyond the limits of legality. The law says, "No adultery." Jesus says, "No lust!" It's not enough to refrain from the overt act; we are not even permitted the mental and emotional act! For "I tell you:" says Jesus, "anyone who looks at a woman and wants to possess her is guilty of committing adultery with her in his heart".

And, as if that weren't strict enough, he adds two even stricter statements: "If your eye causes you to sin, gouge it out! . . . If your hand causes you to sin, cut it off!" First he pushes the definition of sexual impurity back to include our inner feelings, and then he pushes it even further back to include the first look of the eye and the first touch of the hand!

My, how we rush to take the sting out of this idea by giving it all kinds of qualifiers! We're quick to point out, for instance, that Jesus was speaking figuratively in the "eye and hand bit." Also, we note how gentle he was with the woman who was caught in adultery. Then we protest that every virile male cannot help but feel sexual stirrings when he looks upon a member of the fairer sex—not to mention the fact that an unfulfilled sex drive can be destructive to us humans.

Granted, Jesus does speak here in dramatic terms. But that is poor reason to dilute or evade his stern command. The Christian is required to go beyond the legal limits in controlling his sex drive. He is to amputate all of those occasions which would lead him to adultery. To argue that he cannot achieve this is to say that he is a victim of natural urges which he cannot master. That's Freud, not Gospel!

God recognizes our sexual needs; he created them. He has given us a framework for meeting those needs—the family. To argue that we cannot live within that framework is to dispute both experience and our nature as human beings.

I suppose we must speak to the tiresome question of just what constitutes "looking upon a woman to possess her sexually." Was Jesus referring to the feeling we all experience when we see a physically beautiful person? Was he talking about performing a "mental sexual act"? Did he mean inward preoccupation with sexual thoughts? Or what?

I don't know how he would precisely define it. That's really not the point. The point, in my opinion, is that the Christian can and must run his sex drive and not let his sex drive run him. If looking at a woman makes him lose control, don't look! If touching a woman causes the loss of control, don't touch!

Besides, I suspect that most of the people who attempt to split hairs over what Jesus meant in this teaching are really looking for loopholes anyway. I suspect this because I've found myself doing the same thing from time to time!

As I said at the outset, I'm bothered more by the parts of the Sermon I *do* understand than by the parts I don't. And I do understand what Jesus is saying here—namely that controlling one's sex drive means more than simply being legal.

Salt and Light and Divorce

The next example of how a Christian is to be salt and light to his world has to do with divorce (Matt. 5:31–32). The Mosaic law required that a man provide his wife with a written bill of divorcement if he wished to terminate the marriage. This bill enabled her to remarry and resume a normal course in life. The law was established to insure order within the community.

Obviously, the Christian should obey the law. Again, obeying it fits his role as salt/preserver. As was true with the other laws, Jesus doesn't abolish the law of divorce. Instead he "fills it up," or expands it. The Christian is to go beyond what is legally required in society, and to point to God's will in all matters.

What is God's will in this matter? That people should not divorce! Society cannot survive on the dissolution of the family. Later, in Matthew 19, Jesus adds more detail to what he says here. Moses established the law concerning bills of divorcement because many men were deserting their wives and leaving them without legal rights. But God's will is for husbands and wives to stay together and grow together. There is simply no justification for divorce, save perhaps in the case of adultery, and many scholars think that exception was added to the text long after Jesus spoke these words.

So, the law said that if one is going to divorce, he should provide a bill. But Jesus said that his disciples must not divorce.

What are we going to do with this teaching? Obviously, we do not wish to let it stand, with so many divorced persons in our present society. It makes us too nervous. Even as I am writing this, I am sensitive to the fact that very likely the reader is divorced. Does it mean that he is not a Christian, that he is a second-class citizen in the kingdom of God?

Not at all. If violating God's plan for the world excluded us from participating in God's kingdom, none of us could qualify. We all manage to sin, one way or another. There is always forgiveness and the chance for a new beginning, whether it be after a divorce, or adultery, or murder, or anger, or anything else.

I do not wish to condemn anyone or to create unjustified guilt. But I do wish to acknowledge that divorce is at best a failure in the kingdom of God. I do wish to be faithful to what Jesus teaches here. Marriage is no light affair. The hope of the world rests upon the solidarity of the family. Modern pressures upon marriage and the fact that "everyone's doing it" are no legitimate excuses for passing off Jesus' words as being outdated.

Too many couples approach marriage with the attitude that, if the going gets rough, they can always divorce. The Christian approaches marriage with the attitude that divorce is out of the question; therefore, when the going gets rough, he concentrates on overcoming the problem instead of dissolving the relationship.

Easy divorce is simply another symptom of the American obsession with "easy everything." The easy solution to a crowded labor market is forced retirement, whereby we cast the aging onto a junk heap of obsolescence, much as we do with used automobiles. The easy solution to unwanted pregnancies is the abortion of unwanted fetuses. The easy solution to bothersome involvement by government is a nation run by small interest groups.

Divorce is a tragic experience. Those who have endured it do not need additional self-righteous pressure from me. On the other hand, neither can our society long endure, if it does not restore the sanctity of marriage. Jesus' idea may make us uneasy, but it points us to the kingdom of God.

Salt and Light and Oaths

Jesus' next application of the salt-light strategy is to the matter of swearing oaths (Matt. 5:33–37). A discussion of oath-swearing has little meaning to us moderns. We rarely encounter the need for it except in courts of law, or ceremonies where people take public office, or occasionally at weddings.

However, in Jesus' time, oaths were used frequently much in the same way that we sign contracts to cement business dealings. There were several kinds of oaths; a person could "swear by" several objects. He could swear by God, by heaven, by earth, by Jerusalem, or by his own head. If he swore by God, he could not break his word. But there was much debate as to whether he could break his word when he swore by the other witnesses listed above.

Jesus no doubt recognized the need for an oath structure in society. Order cannot be maintained without some mechanism which legally insures that promises will be kept. We must remember again that Jesus said he was not out to erase the laws of the land but to fulfill them. So, Christians are to obey their legal agreements. This is their way of preserving order.

However, Jesus repeats his pattern by pointing us beyond the law once more. The Christian should not swear at all—by God, or heaven, or earth, or Jerusalem, or anything else! Because a Christian is already swearing by God when he says yes or no! When a Christian gives his word, he is giving God's word. He doesn't need oaths to make him keep it. If he lies about anything, he's lying in the name of God!

In other words, Jesus is not abolishing legal agreements here; he is saying that Christians should keep their agreements whether they are legally binding or not. Telling the truth, keeping one's word, is the way the Christian points the world to the kingdom.

One of the most "Christian" businessmen I've ever known is a gentleman named David Barrow. He is in his eighties now and very ill. At the age of forty-nine, he quit a three-thousand-dollar-per-year job and entered real estate development. In the next twenty years, he earned millions. Some of his success was due to being in the right place at the right time, but the chief reason was that the community knew he was a man of his word. If he said "Yes," people knew he meant "yes," and vice versa.

I was describing Mr. Barrow to a friend, who is a professional mountain climber. My friend said, "In my profession we have a saying about men like him: 'He's the guy you want holding the rope.'" He went on to explain that when a climber slipped and fell, the person holding the tether line could save the victim only at a very painful price. The tether would snake through his hands at blinding speed, burning through his gloves and his flesh. It took consummate courage to hold on.

The Christian must keep his legal agreements to preserve the world's order, but he must go beyond what is legally required and hold onto the rope of truth at all costs. In so doing, he is the light which points men to God.

Salt and Light and Enemies

The fifth and final example of the Christian's relationship to his world deals with how we are to relate to our enemies (Matt. 5:38–47). It is an intricate passage, filled with numerous possibilities for embellishment and argument. To give it full treatment would require a book in itself. But as I see it, we must resist the tendency to "go off chasing rabbits" and attempt to read the passage within the context of the salt-light strategy which Jesus has been illustrating all along.

Like all systems of law, the Mosaic Law was concerned with checking the evil which threatened to destroy the unity of society. Its answer was to punish the evildoer in proportion to his offense—an eye for an eye, a tooth for a tooth, a life for a life, and so on. It attempted to strike a just balance between the crime and the punishment.

My feeling is that Jesus accepted the necessity of such a system. Remember, he said that he had not come to abolish the Law of Moses. Society cannot survive if it allows evildoers to go unchallenged. There must be a system which insures the safety of the law-abiding citizen; otherwise, the society breaks down.

Therefore, the Christian's salt-task is to live within the system of justice and thus preserve the order of his society. Of course, if the scales of justice are tipped in favor of either the victim or the criminal, he must protest and work to balance them. But that is another story, and I promised not to "chase rabbits."

The central point is that the Christian must accept the realistic necessity of a system which punishes the lawless and rewards the lawful. Such a system is the only means by which order can be maintained in society. It is naive to think that society can hold together otherwise.

However, as before, Jesus points his disciples beyond the legal necessities of dealing with evildoers to a higher concept. Whereas the Mosaic Law is aimed at punishing evildoers, Jesus' philosophy is aimed at eradicating *the evil itself, but redeeming the evildoer!*

In essence, he's asking us a question regarding how we relate to our enemies. It goes something like this: "When someone does evil to you, what do you want? Do you want to do away with the evil or with the evildoer? If it is the evildoer you want to destroy, the Law of Moses is sufficient. But if you wish to destroy the evil itself and to salvage the evildoer in the process, you must take another approach with your enemy." It is the approach of the one who wants to be a light to his world, a pointer to the kingdom of God. And, I might add, this approach made Jesus' listeners very nervous, just as it does today.

The strategy he teaches can be summarized in two

concepts. First, the only way to destroy the evil and to salvage the evildoer in the process is to *respond in contrast.* Do not respond in kind. Do not return a wrong for a wrong; return a right for a wrong. "If your enemy slaps you on the right cheek, let him slap you on the left cheek also. If someone sues you for your shirt, give him your coat, too. If one of the occupation troops forces you to carry his pack one mile, carry it two. When someone hustles you for money, be gullible and give it to him. When someone wants to borrow something and you're aware that he probably won't repay you, lend it to him" (Matt. 5:39–42).

In our way of thinking, this is absolute madness. We tend to think that the only way to eradicate evil is to give it a dose of its own medicine: Kill the killers, hate the haters, be closed-minded toward the closed-minded, etc.

Throughout history, we have used this method. It is so deeply ingrained in our beings that we resist any suggestion that it could be the best ally the forces of evil have. From international to interpersonal relations, it is considered standard practice to use evil as a weapon against evil. Jesus' response-in-contrast strategy is regarded as cowardly hogwash, or at best logical nonsense. We have yet to put his words into practice, because we have yet to even recognize that what he teaches actually makes sense.

So, first of all, let's compare the logic of Jesus' approach with the logic of the so-called "classic approach" to combating evil. As we said earlier, the classic approach is based upon the notion that evil can be destroyed with evil. If someone does us wrong, we are justified in returning the wrong. Does this rid the world of evil? No! It perhaps rids the world of an evildoer, but the evil has only increased. For now we too are evildoers. Evil has simply found a new residence—*in us!*

I met a former Green Beret from the Viet Nam war who illustrated how evil is transferred rather than destroyed by the classic approach. I was fishing in Alaska (my father paid my way), and Green Beret was the camp's cook. He lived alone in the wilderness most of the time, and could barely tolerate the presence of people. I took it as a personal mission to become his friend, to draw him out of his shell.

After several days, he began to let down his defenses, but I didn't hear what I expected. He was not shell-shocked or battle-fatigued or remorseful. He was from a rural Arkansas background, and had grown up in the church. He had volunteered for duty out of patriotic devotion, and had chosen to serve three successive tours in the combat zone, coming home only because he had been severely wounded on his last tour.

He told me stories which chilled my blood. Twenty-two Viet Cong had died from the knife he showed me with gleaming eyes. He told of assassinating village chieftains in their beds, of strangling South Vietnamese soldiers who had not fought well in battle, and of burning people alive in their huts. But the most chilling account was the one about the pregnant woman.

They had trapped several Viet Cong in a small village, into which they were lobbing mortar shells. The woman was working in a field beside the village, and when she saw her house afire she began to scream incessantly. Her children were in the village.

As the fight raged on, the woman continued to shriek as she stood there helpless in the open field. "That little snit," said the ex–Green Beret, "was driving me nuts! When she wouldn't stop, I thought, 'What the hell, all of them are the same.' . . . So I just up and popped her with a bullet, right in her watermelon belly. She didn't holler no more after that."

I thought of a quote from John Claypool's great

sermon which he delivered following the terrorist attack on the Olympic Village in Munich. It goes something like this: "If in order to defeat the beast, I become the beast, then bestiality reigns." A pastoral lad from Arkansas, raised in a Christian environment, had answered the call of his country to go and defeat the beast. But in order to defeat the beast he had to use the beast's methods, and therefore became the beast himself.

If we use evil to combat evil, evil proliferates. If I gouge out one of your eyes, and you respond by gouging out one of mine, and I respond in kind by gouging out your remaining eye, and so on . . . has evil been eradicated? Is that process logical? It's stupid! It makes no sense at all. Yet we all continue to think of it as the *logical approach* to combating evil!

Well, what about Jesus' approach; does it make any more sense than the classic approach? Not if all we're seeking is personal safety and revenge on the evildoers. But if we're willing to risk our personal safety and to redeem evildoers, it makes a lot of sense. In fact, responding in contrast to our enemies is about the only hope there is for destroying the evil in this world. The classic approach hasn't worked—that's for sure!

Jesus' approach *will* work; we must have the courage to believe that! And we must have the sense to understand that this approach is the duty of those who are the "lights which point to the kingdom." To be his disciple means to respond in contrast to our enemies.

How does Jesus' strategy work? I saw it work one time at a Little League baseball game. I was ten years old. Our third baseman was my best friend, Rudy Castillo. We were playing for the championship of the North Zone of the Houston League. The game had come down to the classic situation—last inning, score tied, bases loaded, two strikes and three balls, Rudy at bat. He singled home the winning run, and we all went crazy. The fans flooded the field; the place was bedlam.

Then the big first baseman from the opposing team—an Anglo boy—strode over to Rudy and through clenched teeth said, "You dirty ——— greaser!" Rudy promptly felled him with a left hook. The lad rolled in the dirt, crying and spitting blood. Everyone associated with either team squared off to do battle.

Rudy's father, a gentle hardworking emigrant from Mexico, spun his son around and stared at him with a mixture of hurt and sadness. "Son," he said, "You just proved that you are exactly what this boy called you." Then he picked up the boy, wiped his face, and hugged him.

We all went home. Response in contrast worked!

And, as Claypool points out in his marvelous sermon, it worked that day at the Cross, too. In the midst of the bloodthirsty mob, there stood a Roman soldier who had witnessed death on a hundred gory battlefields. The execution of criminals was his stock and trade.

Yet when he heard Jesus forgiving his enemies, he was struck through all of the callouses of his being. In awe, he said, "Surely this man is the Son of God!"

What would happen if we dared to live by Jesus' unnerving idea of responding in contrast to our enemies? Many of us would die, to be sure. But then the kingdom of God might come, too.

Thus far, we have described the first part of what Jesus means by being lights in our relationships to our enemies. We are to respond in contrast. Now, we come to the second part which actually is tied to the first. We mentioned this concept earlier in our discussion of "being merciful."

The only way we can muster the capacity to respond

in contrast to our enemies is to recognize that they are as much a part of the human family as we are. This is the gist of Jesus' teaching about "loving our enemies." (Matt. 5:43–47). Listen to his words:

> You have been taught that you should love your friends and hate your enemies. But I tell you, love your enemies and pray for those who persecute you . . . for your heavenly Father makes his sun to shine on bad and good people alike, and gives rain to those who do good and to those who do evil. Why should God reward you, if you love only the people who love you? . . . Even the pagans do that!

God views all people as one family, and he is out to redeem them all. He does not love only those who have responded to his love. He loves the ones who have rejected him as well, just as a father loves his wayward son as much as his obedient son. Even though a wayward son is not at home with the father, he is still a son. That's why "the Father makes his sun to shine on the good and bad alike."

Jesus tells us to take our cue from God in relating to our enemies. For they are our brothers, even though they are our enemies. Only when we recognize this fact can we return good for evil. Only when we see this common humanity does our enemy come to seem worthy of our efforts to redeem him.

The trouble with so much of the Church's evangelism over the years is that it has operated with the assumption that unbelievers are "other" in nature, a subhuman breed. The aim therefore has been to vanquish the unbeliever and bring him into submission. Jesus saw unbelievers as straying members of the one human flock. His effort was not to whip them into submission, but to lead them back home where they belonged.

In short, we cannot love our enemies until we begin to see that they are *not* enemies, but lost brothers. Only then do these words of Jesus make sense: "No greater love hath man than to lay down his life for another."

Thus, the Christian's task is to eradicate evil by making the enemy his friend. That such a notion makes our society nervous hardly needs mentioning. It's not our way, either inside or outside of the church. Nevertheless, it *is* Jesus' way.

The Bottom Line

Jesus finishes his teaching about the Christian's role in society with one short sentence, but that sentence is like the bottom line of a financial statement. It tells all in succinct, stark terms: "Be ye perfect as your Father in heaven is perfect" (Matt. 5:48).

Usually we skip over that one. It is too ridiculous to take seriously—"the X of all Xs." It would help us, however, to know that in the original text Jesus' words read differently. For one thing, he uses progressive verbs. For another, the word translated "perfect" means "mature," "full-grown," "finished." So what Jesus is actually saying is, "Be on your way toward becoming a finished, mature personality like God."

Jesus didn't assume that we could reach sinless perfection; he assumed that we could constantly be progressing toward the image of God. All of his teachings here only condemn and discourage us if we think we can accomplish them in one fell swoop. We were all created with potential to become like God. Our role in the world is to constantly be on the way to that potential.

Gertrude Behanna used to end her Christian testimony with a prayer:

God, I ain't what I ought to be;
But I ain't what I used to be;
And, Praise God, I ain't what I'm gonna' be!

This is the prayer of us all, when it comes to how we are to live in the world.

Summary

I have said that Jesus' ideas about how the Christian is to relate to his world really jangles our nerves. For we have never overcome the "withdraw and keep the Law" strategy. We are still hung up on the notion that the Christian should isolate himself within the sacred sector of his institutions, rituals, and laws.

We have yet to catch up to Jesus' strategy, which I have defined as the "salt and light" strategy. Like salt, the Christian is to penetrate his society and preserve its order. This means obeying the law; Jesus did not come to do away with the Law. But we should go beyond the legal and serve as a light which points men to life in the kingdom of God. Thus, every Christian has his salt-function and his light-function—he preserves and he points; he meets legal requirements, but he goes beyond the merely legal.

Jesus gives five examples of how this strategy works. First, the Christian should obviously refrain from murder. This is his salt-function. But he should also go beyond the legal and refrain from hating. Second, the Christian should not commit adultery; adultery not only is legally wrong, but it also destroys community. However, he should go beyond the law again; he should not lust.

When it comes to divorce, the Christian should obey the laws regulating divorce, but he should go a step further and not divorce at all. Again, he should accept the need for oaths in the everyday world, but he should also regard every *yes* and *no* he utters as though it were an oath in God's name.

The final example regards how the Christian is to relate to his enemies. As salt, he must acknowledge the necessity of some system of justice in society; otherwise, the social order would disintegrate. But, he must go beyond the legal once more, and seek to make his enemy his friend by responding in contrast to his enemy's actions.

Finally, by living beyond the legal, the Christian is in the process of becoming like God.

QUESTIONS FOR STUDY

1. What two words from the Sermon on the Mount best symbolize how the Christian is to relate to his world? Explain what each symbolizes.
2. What is the Christian's responsibility toward the laws of the land?
3. Is it ever right to break a law? Is it right to escape the penalty for doing so?
4. Give the salt-light strategy of the Christian concerning murder, adultery, divorce, and enemies.

CHAPTER THREE

UNNERVING NOTIONS ABOUT PIETY

(Matthew 6:1–18)

Rescuing a Bad Word

Words are like the U.S. dollar—they keep getting devalued so that they don't mean what they used to. For instance, at one time, if you called a woman "homely," you were complimenting her. Now it means she's a plain Jane. *Vulgar* once meant "popular," or "commonly used." Now it means "coarse," or "nasty." *Sin* once meant "rebellion against God"; now it means anything you're doing that I don't like to do, or wish I could do, but don't have either the energy or the nerve to try.

Piety is such a word. There was a time when everyone would have relished being called a pietist. Now we use the word to describe the kind of Christian we abhor. As a teenager once told me, "A pietist is a hypocritical, pompous ass who looks as though he were weaned on milk of magnesia."

There is a comedian who has become quite famous because of a single routine which he repeats over and over. His stage name is Raymond J. Johnson, Jr. The straight man makes a point to address him as "Mr. Johnson," which prompts him to launch into the routine: "Oh! You doesn't has to call me Johnson!" he says. "You can call me Ray! Or you can call me Jay! Or you can call me Ray Jay! Or you can call me Ray Jay Junior! But you doesn't has to call me Johnson!"

We Christians react similarly when we're called "pious." You can call me "dedicated," or you can call me "committed," or you can call me "devoted." But don't call me "pious"!

In spite of our aversion to the word, I should like to rescue *piety,* because I think it best fits the context of Jesus' teaching in the third section of the Sermon on

the Mount. I would define piety as the devout fulfillment of all religious obligations. It includes any and
everything we do out of religious motivation: worship,
prayer, meditation, Bible study, evangelism, mission
work, and monetary giving.

Piety, for God's Sake

Jesus had some disturbing ideas about piety, the chief
one being that piety is primarily for God's sake and his
alone. Every religious act should be aimed first at
enhancing God's standing in the world. *Piety is primarily
for God—not for ourselves, not for others, not for society!*
This made Jesus' listeners edgy, because they had
been reared to believe that piety was aimed at enhancing *their standing* before God and before others. The
chief reason for practicing religion was to earn God's
approval and to be highly regarded in the world. In
short, piety had become a self-serving enterprise.

It is not difficult to see how such an attitude occurs.
All piety has a way of becoming organized into standard modes and rituals which are passed from one
generation to the next. Whether or not we are aware of
it, we practice religion according to a pattern. It may be
a formalized pattern, written down and organized into
precise rituals. Or it may simply be an unwritten,
traditional "way of doing things."

As time passes, we tend to follow the pattern, but to
forget what it's supposed to accomplish. Someone said
of Columbus' discovery of America, "When he set out,
he didn't know where he was going. When he got there,
he didn't know where he was. When he returned, he
didn't know where he had been." That's the way many
of us regard our religious practices. We go through the
motions, but we don't know the "what for."

When this vacuum of purpose occurs, we are likely to fill it by using our piety to serve ourselves. That's what happened to the people of Jesus' day. They lost sight of the fact that the purpose of piety is to enhance God, so they used it to enhance themselves.

Isn't the same true today? Why do we worship, pray, study, etc.—to enhance our own standing before God and others, or to enhance God's standing in the world?

Several years ago, I participated in a conference which was led by some of the most prominent religious spokesmen in America. Writers, teachers, and preachers from every segment of the religious community were present. It was a "star-studded cast."

At one point, the purpose of worship was the focal topic. A leading mystic defined it as, "making love to God." He went on to explain his meaning: "When we worship," he said, "first, we have to get in the mood." He described how his congregation went through several conditioning exercises to create "the mood." They meditated upon writings; they touched each other; several gave "love testimonies" toward God and each other; music was performed; chants in unison followed. Everything built toward a state of ecstasy, at which point the Holy Spirit was said to enter the service.

At this point, our speaker interjected the belief that God really doesn't need our worship, because he is a self-contained God. Therefore, "Worship is not for God, but for us! Worship is a matter of recharging our spiritual batteries by eliciting God's love in the moment."

The next speaker was a leading Protestant pastor. He took the mystic to task. "Worship," he said, "is not for us; it's *for God!* The purpose of worship is to honor him and him alone. It is not a question of whether God needs or doesn't need our worship. We do not worship in order to meet God's needs or ours. We worship in order to establish God's reign in the world!"

The third speaker was a renowned professor of theology. The stage had been set. Two opposing views had been cast before the group. One said that worship is for man; the other said that worship is for God.

The professor came on with an air of loving conciliation. He showed the merits of each side of the argument and concluded that worship is *both for man and for God*. Everyone applauded, the mystic and the pastor shook hands warmly, and a feeling of accomplishment was shared by all.

Little did we realize that we had become the victims of an age-old fallacy among Christians. We had evaded the truth for the sake of nicety and conciliation. We were more interested in reaching agreement among ourselves than in reaching the truth about the purpose of worship.

Although the pastor's view of worship was closest to what Jesus says in the Sermon on the Mount, we couldn't hear him because of the conflict that existed between his view and the mystic's view. Both were such nice, devoted fellows that we felt compelled to find a mediating position which would do both of them credit.

The truth is that worship, like all piety, is *for God's sake*. We do not worship for what we can get out of it, but for what God's kingdom can get out of it.

I have made it a point to conduct a survey in each of the five churches I've served in the past twenty years, asking the members to indicate why they come to church. In every case, the answers have varied widely, but they all share a common motif. First, let's look at the answers which are most often given, and then talk about the motif.

To the question, "Why do you come to church?" the most frequently given answers are: (1) To feel God's presence; (2) To learn more about God; (3) To be with my Christian friends; (4) To give my children a Christian environment; (5) To gain the strength to face life weekly; (6) To keep myself morally pure; (7) For the preaching; (8) For the music; (9) For the Bible study; (10) It's just something I've always done; (11) It makes me feel good.

Rarely have I found answers which are not included in the above. What do these responses say about our piety? Obviously, that for a great number of Christians, piety is a self-serving enterprise! It is primarily designed to enhance one's standing before God and men. It is designed for the purpose of receiving, not giving!

Let's face it, most people go to church much in the same way as they go to a mechanic when their car is broken, or to a physician when they are ill. That is, they go in order to have their needs cared for. As someone has said, the Church is a "covenant of personal concerns, not a covenant of servants who have united to transform the world."

Perhaps we should inject here that there's nothing wrong with embracing God out of personal need. After all, where else can a person go when he is broken? The Bible does picture Jesus as the Great Physician, and he *did* say, "Come unto me, all of you who are heavy laden, and I will give you rest" (Matt. 11:28).

There is nothing wrong with turning to God out of personal concern; but here is where the disturbing part comes in: *The church is not God! It is not a hospital where one goes to be healed! The church is a fellowship of persons who have already been healed!*

People do not go to church in order to be healed; they go to church because they have been healed by the grace of God and have resolved to join with the healed in order to heal the world!

In short, one goes to *Jesus Christ* to be healed, and he unites with the *Church* in order to heal others! That notion makes us so nervous that we don't even like to think about it. Yet I am convinced that it is what Jesus thought. Piety is not for us; it's for the kingdom of God.

A close examination of the text bears this out. Remember, Jesus is speaking to his disciples, not to the crowd. He's talking to those who have already entered the kingdom, to those who have already been healed.

He states the central point at the outset: "Do not practice your piety in order to gain the praise of men. If you do, you will not be rewarded by God" (Matt. 6:1). This theme recurs throughout the section which follows. If we practice our piety in order to help ourselves and not God, our efforts are useless.

Then Jesus chooses three contemporary practices of piety to illustrate his point: giving money to religious causes, praying, and fasting.

For God's Sake, Give

"When you give your money," he says, "do not sound a trumpet in advance, like the hypocrites in the synagogue and the streets do, in order to receive the praise of onlookers. Instead, give so secretively that your left hand doesn't even know what your right hand is doing. And God alone will see it and will bring the reward out in the open."

The good that our money does should magnify God, and not us—that's the message. We do not give in order to receive anything. We give in order to enhance the kingdom. Piety is for God, not for us.

Anyone who is related to a church knows that the

subject of money is one of the most potentially divisive subjects in Christendom. He also knows that almost every church is forced to depend upon a handful of members to support its budget. Keeping the church afloat financially creates more gray hairs in the pastor's scalp than any other part of his ministry. The truth is that most church members do not contribute appreciably to their churches. And if the government were to remove contributions from tax-exempt status, the result would be a disaster for institutional Christianity.

If there is one area in which I have made the most mistakes as a pastor, it is in the area of motivating people to give their money to the church. Over the years, I have used all of the weapons in the "ministerial arsenal." There's the "God's gonna get you for that" approach, in which the idea is to convince the people that, if they don't give, God will see to it that they will lose the money some other way—usually a painful way.

Then, there's the "shame on you" approach, in which the minister points out that the church is being supported by a few faithful brothers and sisters, and that the majority are really "parking on someone else's nickel." You also throw in little grabbers like, "If God gave you 10 percent of what you gave him last year, could you live on it?" or "If you were on trial for contributing to the church, would there be enough evidence to convict you?"

Another method can be labelled the "you're not gonna let George beat you?" approach. Everyone who has pledged is given a lapel button which says, "I did it." He wears it to Sunday service. Every church group is given a quota, which is posted in an obvious place and arranged with a "fill-in" showing the progress of the group toward their goal.

All of this would be funny if it weren't so sad, if I

hadn't tried it, and if it didn't indicate how blind we are
to the real reason Christians do not give their money to
the church.

The real reason is that we are all part of a system
which views the expenditure of money solely on the
basis of expected return. Money equals "investment."
We spend only if we can receive something in return.

So if the church is a place to which I go in order to
have my personal concerns met, I give only in proportion as I have received. If the church has met my needs
sufficiently, then I give. If it hasn't, I don't.

And of course, I'm always on the lookout for a "good
deal," that is, an opportunity to get something for
nothing. After all, that's what it's all about, isn't it—
getting the most for my investment. If I can enjoy what
someone else pays for, I'd be foolish not to capitalize!

In other words, money problems in the church stem
from the confusion which we noted earlier—the confusion between the church and God. The Christian is
called to give his money to enhance God's reign in the
world, not to support an institution which will meet his
personal concerns.

Jesus taught the principle of *divestment*, not *investment*.
The Christian's task is to *give away* himself and his
possessions to speed the kingdom's coming. Unfortunately, most of us believe the Christian's task is to
invest, in order to receive a profit. But piety is for God's
sake, not ours. That's why Jesus warned us to keep our
giving a secret. For when we do so, the benefits go to
God, not to us.

For God's Sake, Pray

Jesus gives a second illustration to show how our
piety is to be for God's sake. "When you pray," he says,
"don't do as the hypocrites who like to stand before the

synagogue and in the streets so men can hear them. They already have what they are after. When you pray, go into your private room, and having shut the door, pray to God in secret, and God who sees in secret will render to you openly" (Matt. 6:5–6).

As in the case of giving our money, we are to pray not for our benefit, but for God's. This becomes even clearer as Jesus continues. He tells us not to use empty repetitions, thinking that the longer our prayers, the more they will be heard. God doesn't need a hearing aid or an update on our needs. He already knows what we need before we pray (Matt. 6:7–8).

In other words, praying is not a self-serving exercise. Its aim is not to enhance our standing with the world or with God. Jesus is continuing the same piety theme we've been talking about all along. Prayer, like worship, is for God's sake.

To show what he means by praying for God's sake, Jesus gives us an example of how we should pray. We call this example "The Lord's Prayer," although perhaps it would be more appropriate to call it "The Disciple's Prayer," since it was given to the disciples as a model for prayer.

The theme of this model prayer is the kingdom of God. It begins, "Our Father, who art in heaven, sanctified be thy name. Thy kingdom come, thy will be done on earth as in heaven." According to Jesus' model, praying for God's sake means praying for the establishment of the kingdom on earth and praying that God will be acknowledged on earth the way he is acknowledged in heaven.

The remainder of the model prayer consists of what the Christian disciple is to ask for himself—the basic necessities of life, the grace to forgive as God has forgiven us, and the power to withstand the temptations which would deter us from our task. Why should he ask these things for himself—so that he will have a comfortable life? No! Because, as the original reads, "Thine is the only kingdom, and the only glory which lasts throughout all the ages"!

Praying should be praying for God's kingdom to come and for our own effectiveness in helping bring it about. That's all Jesus says about prayer at this point.

Compare *that* to the praying most of us do! Why do we pray? Mostly for our own security, I suspect. The evil from which we want to be delivered is not the evil which keeps us from enhancing the kingdom, but the evil which threatens our comfort in this world.

Furthermore, do we pray for the basic physical necessities, or for luxuries? Or do we even know the difference!

I visited recently with a man who has made millions in the electronic computer business. His is a classic Horatio Alger story. I asked him how he happened to get in on the ground floor of the computer boom and become one of the world's richest men. "When I was a boy, I read a lot about Henry Ford," he said. "Mr. Ford said that when he chose the automobile industry as a career, the auto was a luxury. However, he foresaw that what was then regarded as a luxury could one day be made into a necessity. So he simply set out to make a luxury into a necessity."

The man continued: "I took my clue from Mr. Ford and began to look around for a luxury which I could turn into a necessity. The electronic computer fit the bill!"

Most of today's necessities were at one time luxuries—automatic dishwashers, clothes dryers, air conditioners, etc. We can't tell the difference any more. And this confusion shows up in our praying, I suspect.

Actually, prayer boils down to a very basic issue—whether or not we believe God has enough in his storehouse to care for our basic needs. It's really a matter of our faith in God to care for us. If we trust him, we don't need to pray for things beyond the basics. If we don't trust him, we shall find ourselves praying endlessly for this and that and that and that.

Also, compare what Jesus says about vain repetitions and lengthy prayers to the praying we do. Have you noticed how some people assume a "stage voice" when they pray in public? Either we don't think God understands straight talk, or we're afraid he won't accept prayers offered in everyday street language.

Dr. Gaston Foote, the long-time pastor of the First United Methodist Church in Fort Worth, Texas, spoke at the seminary where I was a student. At the end, he quoted the old Mark Twain prayer: "Father, help us to live such lives that when we die even the undertaker will be sorry." For days, the student body was indignant at his "irreverence in the presence of God." I was part of that "righteous protest."

However, as the years have passed, I have come to appreciate Dr. Foote's prayer, and I suspect that God got a chuckle out of it, too. For none of us considered at the time those prayers delivered day after day at the seminary, which droned with the same tiresome, repetitive, rarefied language and tone. We didn't consider that we seldom heard a prayer that didn't include, "Bless our hearts and our minds."

To pray to live a life whose termination would grieve even the undertaker is not all that far away from what Jesus teaches about prayer in this passage. For that kind of life, indeed, would make a difference for the kingdom of God.

For God's Sake, Fast

Giving is for God's sake, praying is for God's sake, and fasting, Jesus adds, is also for God's sake. "When you fast, don't be like the hypocrites—down in the mouth—for they disfigure their faces so that people will know they are fasting. I tell you, they have already received what they are after. When you fast, comb your hair and wash your face so that you don't look like you're fasting. Let your Father in heaven be the only one who sees you fast. Then the benefit will go to him." (Matt. 6:16–18).

Either most Christians follow Jesus' instructions, or very few Christians fast nowadays, because we rarely hear of the practice any more. From the look of our waistlines, I would suspect that the latter is the case.

Nevertheless, fasting was a great mark of piety in the Jewish religion. I suppose a good modern analogy would be the Christian who goes out of his way to look plain and deprived as a result of his dedication to God. Many Christians seem to equate a stiff, somber countenance with authentic devotion. From this assumption, they evidently come to the additional belief that anything which is hilariously fun is also sinful. They seem to follow the tradition of the medieval priest who instructed Christian young ladies to "weep often and meditate much upon your sins."

Because fasting is perhaps peculiar to so many of us, I would consider it as a part of all those needs of which we deprive ourselves out of religious devotion—a job promotion, a style of clothing, a social activity, etc.

As before, Jesus says that such deprivations are for God's sake and not ours. We are not to deprive ourselves in order to earn "brownie points" with God or with men. The only legitimate reason for self-denial is to effect the kingdom of God among men. If God receives the benefit, self-denial is authentic; if we receive the benefit, it is not.

Why for God's Sake?

You may have been asking, "Why was Jesus so adamant about our piety being primarily for God's sake? Isn't this rather selfish on God's part? And what about piety for the sake of others? The Bible urges us to practice our piety for the benefit of our fellow-man, doesn't it?

I believe the answer to these questions is that piety can ultimately benefit ourselves and others *only if it is aimed at helping God first.*

The only way our piety can help us and others is for it to be motivated by the desire to glorify God. It is only through glorifying God that we can become what we were meant to be and can help others become what they were meant to be.

This may seem like a roundabout way of making piety a self-serving practice, but there is a difference between piety for self's sake and piety for God's sake. The difference is one of motive, as I hope our discussion has shown. If our motive is to help ourselves by being pious, then piety becomes an occasion for pride. Jesus pointed this out in the story he told about the Pharisee and the tax collector who went to the Temple to pray. "How proud I am, that I am not as other men," said the Pharisee. "I am pious—I am not greedy or immoral, I fast two days a week, and I tithe my income." The Pharisee's piety only produced pride. But piety for God's sake produced humility, as in the case of the tax collector. He was practicing piety, too. But his prayer was for God's mercy.

Why must piety be for God's sake? Because piety for God's sake is the only means by which we can avert pride. However, there is a second reason: piety for God's sake is the *only way we can keep from being molded by our cultural environment.*

The perennial sin of all Christians is that they allow their culture to shape them, rather than shaping their culture. And the chief reason is that they become interested in gaining this culture's approval instead of standing up to it and challenging its values. When this happens, piety becomes a mechanism for gaining the world's praise instead of an instrument for changing the world's values.

Several years ago, a study in California purported to show that a person's affiliation with a church made very little difference when it came to racial discrimination. In fact, the study held that in many instances the churchgoers were more prejudiced than the non-churchgoers. Two researchers, named Campbell and Fukiyama, did an analysis of a questionnaire sent to eight thousand members of the United Church of Christ to determine whether the California study was indeed accurate. The result of their analysis was a book entitled, *The Fragmented Layman.*

Campbell and Fukiyama were surprised to find that the charges made by the California study were to a large extent true. Churchgoers are as racially preju-diced as nonchurchgoers, if not more so. However, the two authors made one key qualification. Recognizing that there are all sorts of reasons people go to church, they divided the churchgoers into four categories. Some churchmen are *organizationally oriented;* they embrace the church in order to participate in some activity sponsored by the Church. Others are *belief oriented;* they are in the church in order to protect it from corruption, and are therefore usually doctrinaire and dogmatic. There are those who are *intellectually oriented;* they see religion as a "head-trip," a studious quest.

The fourth group of churchgoers are *devotionally oriented*. They have two distinctive traits. First, they have a deep personal sense of relationship to a living God. Everything they do in life is sensitive to this personal relationship. Second, they see themselves as being part of a grand scheme to transform the world according to God's prescriptions.

Now, get this: Campbell and Fukiyama discovered that the first three types mentioned above exhibited racial attitudes which were unaffected by their religious piety. But the devotionally oriented churchgoers were different! They alone were the kind of church members who "reversed social conditioning rather than reinforcing it."[1]

Now is it clear why piety must be for God's sake? Unless we are devotionally oriented—that is, personally related to God and practicing our piety in order to enhance the kingdom—we cannot resist being swallowed up by the values of our culture. That is precisely why Jesus told his disciples to practice their piety in secret.

Summary

Our thesis in this chapter has been that Jesus held some ideas about piety which were unnerving to his contemporaries and still are. We have used the word *piety* to mean everything one does in order to fulfill his religious obligations.

Jesus' most disturbing notion regarding piety is that it is to be for God's sake and not the Christian's. This means, in essence, that all religious efforts should be aimed at enhancing and effectuating God's plan to redeem the world. In other words, piety is for bringing in the kingdom of God.

This idea made Jesus' listeners nervous because the

religious folk thought piety was designed to enhance their standing before God and the world. My contention is that the same is true with most Christians today; they practice religion primarily in order to receive rather than to give. They see the Church as a hospital where one goes to receive healing.

Jesus' idea was that one goes to God in order to be healed, and that he goes to the church, *afterward,* in order to become part of God's healing forces in the world. In other words, people go to church because they are healed and want to become healers.

An examination of the text of the Sermon on the Mount bears out this thesis. Jesus begins by stating a principle: If piety is practiced in order to help oneself, it brings no reward from God; it is useless. Then he applies this principle to three instances of piety—giving money to religious causes, praying, and fasting. We are to give our money to help God, not ourselves. Giving is for God's sake. But that's not the way most Christians see it. They see giving as *investment,* not *divestment;* they give in order to receive a profitable return.

Prayer is also to be done for God's sake. We are to pray for the kingdom to come and for the power to be effective instruments in bringing it about. Again, this idea makes us nervous, because we tend to see prayer as a self-serving exercise.

Jesus repeats the same theme with regard to fasting. It too is to be for God's sake, not ours. Fasting is a self-denial exercise. It is one of those exercises in which we deny our wants for the sake of God. If we deny ourselves in order to gain "brownie points" with either God or men, we have missed the whole point of self-denial.

Finally, why should piety be for God's sake? There are two reasons: It is the only way to avoid becoming proud of our piety, and it is the only way to avoid being conditioned by the culture around us.

QUESTIONS FOR STUDY

1. What does the word *piety* mean?
2. According to Jesus, what is the purpose of piety?
3. What is the primary fallacy concerning the purpose of piety in the modern religious world?
4. What three religious practices did Jesus address in the Sermon on the Mount in order to illustrate his teaching concerning piety?
5. What are the two chief reasons for demanding that all piety be for God's sake?

CHAPTER FOUR

UNNERVING NOTIONS ABOUT WEALTH

(Matthew 6:19–34)

Don't Be Had by What You Have

Some years ago, a graduate student in California wrote a doctoral thesis in which he contended that a person's value system is revealed by what he throws away. For several months he analyzed the garbage of a number of notable persons in government, business, and entertainment. What they discarded supposedly revealed their values.

That's a novel idea. In a sense, we *are* what we throw away. But I think the other side of the idea is even more true—*we are what we store up*. If you want to get a fix on a person's values, look at what he hoards.

This is the key truth in Jesus' teaching about material possessions in the Sermon on the Mount (Matt. 6:19–34). Unless we remember this principle throughout our study, we shall miss that which makes his ideas about wealth X-rated.

Often we make the mistake of thinking that Jesus condemned wealth and equated being a Christian with taking a vow of poverty. That is, we tend to think that only the Have-nots can find favor with God. In fact, Jesus never said that being rich is wrong; he said that it's dangerous.

In recent times there has arisen a kind of "Robin Hood spirit" in America which would endorse the right of the poor to steal from the rich. For years it was considered a "sin" to be poor; now it's considered a "sin" to be rich.

Obviously, there is a certain justification for this spirit. The distribution of wealth in this country is appalling. The vast majority of the holdings are controlled by a handful, and they get richer while the poor get poorer. The hard facts are that the top one-fifth of the population controls forty percent of the wealth, while the bottom one-fifth controls less than five percent.[1] Also, the majority of the tax burden is shouldered by those three-fifths who fall in the middle!

There's no way to justify this kind of disparity. It's wrong and must be changed. However, the question is, "Changed to what?" What do we Have-nots want? Do we really want to put an end to the gluttony which a few enjoy, or do we want to join the Gluttony Club ourselves? I suspect that underlying this "Robin Hood spirit" there may be a materialistic lust which is every bit as strong as that we attribute to the Haves!

After all, a poor person can be just as materialistic as a rich one! Gluttony is a sin, but so is envy. Dorothy Sayers noted a long time ago that we all begin by asking, "Why should I not enjoy what others enjoy?" and end up demanding, "Why should others enjoy what I may not?"[2]

Is our protest against a society which judges human worth in terms of material possession, or is it, as Saul Alinsky once noted, a cry for a "fatter piece of those decadent, degenerate, bankrupt, materialistic, bourgeois values" which the Haves enjoy?[3]

I'm trying to say that we miss the point of Jesus' view of wealth if we think of it in terms of "Haves vs. Have-nots." He neither condemned nor blessed being rich or poor. His message was directed to the entire economic scale.

And what was the crux of his message? I like to put it this way: *Don't be had by what you have!* Or, if you wish to reverse it, *Don't be had by what you don't have!* Either way, it means the same thing: *Don't allow material possessions to determine your self-image.*

You see, the real danger of materialism is that we tend to view the objects we own as extensions of ourselves. We allow what we have to tell us who and what we are. That's why we react violently when something we have is about to be taken from us.

Being had by what I have means letting my possessions determine who I am. It means letting my Cadillac tell me that I am "successful upper-class" . . . letting my station wagon tell me that I'm "middle-American" . . . letting my jalopy tell me that I'm an underachiever. Letting a custom-built mansion tell me that I'm somebody and letting my shack tell me that I'm a nobody.

The question Jesus seems to be asking is, "Can you *be,* irrespective of what you *have?* Do you have to *have* in order to be somebody? If you lost everything you possess, could you be anybody?"

As we noted earlier, Jesus puts the questions to us within the context of hoarding our wealth. I think he focuses on hoarding because it is the chief symptom of a person who is being had by what he has. In other words, the telltale sign of the person who lets his self-image be determined by what he owns is the hoarding, accumulating, and amassing of things.

Paul Tillich spoke of "thingification" as our real sin against God. Thingification is our turning away from God to the *things* God has created in order to find fulfillment. Paul, in the first chapter of Romans, notes this basic shift of allegiance when he says, "They [mankind] worship and serve what God has created instead of the Creator himself" (Rom. 1:25b).

The essence of all sin is trusting in the "made" instead of the "Maker." When the "made" becomes our ultimate concern, says Tillich, we become consumed with accumulating more and more things. Ultimately, we find ourselves touching things in order to determine whether we exist, not to determine whether the things exist.

I call this process, "being had by what you have," letting things and the number of them which you possess determine your existence.

To summarize: Jesus approached the subject of wealth by warning his disciples not to hoard their possessions. But he focused upon hoarding because it is the evidence of our chief underlying sin—namely, the effort to look for life's meaning in material things.

This made people nervous in Jesus' day. In the first century religious world, wealth was considered a mark of God's favor. Financial reversal was still construed as divine punishment, just as it had been earlier, in the time of Job. When a wealthy person went broke, he was thought to have displeased God. The reverse was also true; if a person prospered materially, he was thought to be in the good graces of God. Of course, the result of this way of thinking was that a person's human worth could be measured by the sum total of his assets.

In spite of our arguments to the contrary, the same still holds true in our society. Like it or not, people are still judged by their productivity and financial position—*in the church as well as outside the church!* We are virtually unable to separate self-worth from financial worth, either in evaluating ourselves or others.

I know a pastor who came to a dying church in one of the largest cities in the country, and under whose leadership the church became one of the largest in the world in five years. He told me his chief strategy at the beginning of his work was to place only successful businessmen in positions of leadership. "They think big, and they know how to get things done," he said. "The mention of a hundred thousand dollars doesn't send them into panic. It may sound suspect, but the truth is, if you want to save a dying church, you've got to go with the moneyed people. Those who work for a living will kill you."

He must have sensed my feelings, for he injected a quick cover-up. "Now God loves everybody, and everybody has a place in the church—I know that," he said. "But you've got to face pragmatic realities. Most people are born followers, and only a few are leaders. And the leaders are the ones who have the bread. So let them lead."

The pragmatism of his argument may be sound, but the philosophy behind it is scary. For instance, it fails to address the question of how the rich leaders became rich! Was the work they did good work? Did it contribute to the betterment of mankind? When they invested their money, did they ask themselves whether the enterprise represented anything useful, or whether it merely represented a safe and profitable return? Did any of them ever refuse money on the grounds that the work they did for it was not honest work?

That "great church" has supported and initiated many worthy causes. It has founded societies to challenge sexual immorality and abstention from alcohol. But I haven't heard of its establishing a society to deal with financial immorality or abstention from usury!

My aim here is not to condemn a particular church— God knows, this particular church has done far more good than bad, and no one is perfect. What I'm trying to speak to is the fact that we still evaluate human worth in terms of financial prowess.

We are a society which, in spite of arguments to the contrary, has not yet escaped the belief that the good life must be preceded by a dollar sign. In short, we are being had by what we have, or by what we don't have. The result is an obsession with accumulating more and

more, with hoarding things and judging our worth by
the size of the cache.

Save for a Sunny Day

Jesus offers us an alternative to the kind of tyranny
described above. He offers us a way to reach fulfillment
regardless of the size of our financial statement. In
short, he gives us a way to keep from being had by what
we have.

In essence, he tells us to "save for a sunny day." We
humans are hoarders by nature. We save things; we
store up material reserves against the unknowns of the
future. We call this "saving for a rainy day." Why?
Because one of our deepest needs is security.

But what is security? I mean ultimately, that is, aside
from the obvious desire to be free from the threat of
harm? Isn't the desire for security really the desire for
permanent existence. Isn't it really the desire to "stay in
one piece" throughout all of the crises which may
threaten our existence? In other words, don't we really
want an *integrated self* which cannot be shattered, no
matter what happens to us?

Thus the craving for security is really the craving for
an "eternal identity." That's because our greatest fear is
the fear of ceasing to exist. Every human fear rests
upon one basic fear—the fear of nothingness. Or, *as it is
often said, the most basic human instinct is self-preservation.*

So we humans are hoarders by nature. And the
reason we do so is self-preservation. We want immortality!

But the tragic thing is that we delude ourselves into
thinking that self can be preserved eternally by storing
up material goods. Somehow we believe that we can
endure throughout the future, if only we can surround
ourselves with enough of the material.

Little do we realize that it is not really *more things* we want, *but the immortality which we think the things will bring us!* A long time ago, St. Augustine knew the truth about us when he said, "Oh God, thou has created us for thyself, and we are restless until we find our rest in Thee!"

Why does a man have five daughters to whom he cannot possibly give enough of his time, and still keep trying to have a son? Because he knows the daughters will not carry on his name after he's dead! Why does a man work himself to death building a material empire which demands so much of him that he cannot enjoy life? He wants "to leave something behind"—an *eternal imprint* upon the world.

Why does a mother push her daughter incessantly to become "Little Miss Everything" and the wife of a moneyed family? Through the daughter, she wants to achieve an "immortality" which she was unable to achieve herself.

We hoard wealth because we want immortality. I love that anecdote about the wealthy woman who arranged to be buried sitting up in a solid gold Cadillac, wearing a half-million dollars worth of furs and jewels. Her wishes were granted. After the funeral, two old grave-diggers came to cover the opulent remains. With a wistful eye, one pointed to the corpse in the Cadillac, sighed, and said to the other, "Man, *that's livin'!*"

"Save for a rainy day," that's our motto. And it means: *accumulate things* in order to assure the survival of the self against all which threatens to destroy its existence.

However, as we said, Jesus' advice is, "Save for a sunny day." He understood our basic hunger for immortality and the attendant need to store up something to insure it. He doesn't tell us not to save; rather, he tells us to *save for the right thing*. We have a basic choice—to store up treasures on earth or treasures in heaven. Earthly treasures cannot last; they are subject to the processes of disintegration ("moths" and "thieves"). So if we're trying to preserve the self by amassing corruptible things, the self dies with the things!

We often hear the adage, "You can't take it with you." Jesus reverses it: "You can't take *you* with *it!*" The self cannot survive on the material. Man cannot live by bread alone.

Heavenly treasures are all that last. "To save for a sunny day" means to invest our lives in the kingdom of God, to save for the day of the Lord. The immortality we crave can be had only by saving for the day which God is bringing; God's "sunny day" is the only durable day there is.

The question is, what's involved in "saving for a sunny day"? How does one invest himself in the kingdom which is to come? By following all of the commands which Jesus has previously given in the Sermon! Saving for a sunny day means following the path to happiness which he outlined in the Beatitudes. It means going beyond the law by following the salt-light strategy in relating to the world. It means practicing the piety which he has prescribed. *In one sense, the Sermon on the Mount is a manual for the eternal survival of the self!* It presents us at every turn with the choice of looking to the world or looking to the kingdom for self-fulfillment. Thingification or glorification, treasures on earth or treasures in heaven—these are the choices upon which our happiness, our labor, and our self-integration rest. These are the basic issues of life itself.

Another thing needs to be said immediately. We cannot save for the sunny day of the Lord—that is, we cannot store up treasures in the kingdom—unless we have already had a glimpse of the kingdom. (I reiterate: the Sermon was directed to Jesus' disciples, not to the crowd.) No one can afford to risk investing in the kingdom until he's experienced it.

We are really pointing to the difference between one who is "saved" and one who is "unsaved." To be saved is to receive a foretaste of the kingdom. The only *essential difference* between a Christian and a non-Christian is that the former has foretasted the kingdom, while the latter has not. We of course would like to think otherwise, but this is the essence of the matter.

This essential difference explains why so many people attempt to insure their immortality through the material. They haven't seen the kingdom! They don't know what the Christian knows! The kingdom of earth is the only kingdom they know; therefore, it's the only kingdom in which they are investing. Perhaps I should add that many of them are also church members.

Let us come back to the point at hand—namely, that only those who have experienced the kingdom can invest in the kingdom. Otherwise, Jesus' words appear to be pure nonsense. I'm reminded of the guy whose wife owned a cat which he despised. She loved that cat with a passion—combed it, washed it, fed it, and pampered it. He was allergic to cat hair, hated the litter box, was incensed by the scratch marks on the furniture, and couldn't sleep at night for the cat's incessant purring.

One evening while his wife slept he took the cat out and drowned it. Then he slipped back in without awakening the wife. Next day, she was shattered by grief when she discovered that the cat was missing.

To show his husbandly concern, he posted a five-hundred-dollar reward for the cat's safe return! One of his friends said, "Five hundred dollars! Man, you must be nuts; no cat is worth that much! What will you do if someone shows up with the cat?"

"When you know what I know," the man said, "You can afford to take the risk!"

Knowing what he knows, the Christian can afford the risk of storing up his treasures in the kingdom. But if he doesn't know, he cannot afford to take the risk. We only risk our existence on that which we feel is durable.

I think that's what Jesus is referring to in his concluding sentence concerning storing treasures in heaven. He says, "Your heart will always be where your treasure is" (Matt. 6:21). The word *heart* here means dedication, the deepest kind of dedication, the kind of dedication to which we refer when we say, "put your *heart* into it," or "Give it 100 percent."

Our deepest dedication is to that which we know will give us life. Our dedication is where our treasure is. That's a sobering thought whenever we begin to check out what it is to which we're giving 100 percent.

With One Eye You Can See the Forever

Jesus has said that the way to keep from being had by what we have is to invest our lives in the kingdom—a process we have described as "saving for a sunny day." Theoretically, this makes sense. But practically speaking, we all know that it's well-nigh impossible to constantly keep our values straight. Even though we've tasted the kingdom which is to come, we keep getting sucked back into the sponge of materialism.

When I decided to pursue the ministry at the age of twenty, I knew that future material prosperity would be off-limits. At the time, I didn't care. I had recently "tasted the kingdom" for the first time; money was not important. For several years I pastored small congregations and barely subsisted.

I remember well that parsonage in which we were forced to let our baby sleep with us, for fear that she would be bitten by rats if she slept alone. I trapped twenty-six of the critters in one night! The water was so bad that we had to boil it for drinking and lace it with Pine O'Pine for bathing.

My salary was thirty dollars per week. I supplemented it by baling hay and clearing brush with an axe for thirty-five cents an hour, fourteen hours a day. This was not in the "old days," either; it was in 1961.

About a year ago, my wife and I drove by that country church. As we sat in the car, I asked what was her most distinctive memory about our years there. Now understand—Lois rarely uses profanity of any kind. But this time she said, "My most distinctive memory? Let's see . . . They had the skinniest damned chickens in the whole world!"

We went on reminiscing about how far we'd come since those days. Now we have a lovely house of our own, atop a mountain and overlooking a lake. We have two cars and a jeep. We enjoy a salary which is near the top of the scale of ministerial salaries.

Not long after our visit to the former church, we began to be criticized for our materialistic lifestyle. The criticism prompted us immediately to defend ourselves by harking back to stories about rats, and dirty water, and hay baling, and brush clearing, and skinny chickens! We were righteously indignant toward our accusers. "Why, the very idea!" we said, "Let me tell you, I paid my dues! I *deserve* everything I have and more! I went to school as long as a medical doctor! The work I do is good work! Besides, you are just jealous, anyway! You're part of that insidious group which believes that the best way to keep the preacher humble is to keep him poor!"

The very idea of being accused of materialism was

something we couldn't fathom. For several months we stewed and agonized over the charges. The more I thought about it, the angrier I became. My whole attitude toward my congregation changed. I became paranoid, living a guarded life and allowing no one into my confidence. Slowly, I developed a disdain for all of my ministerial duties. It seemed that everything I did was designed to prove that I was worth what I was being paid.

Then one day I was looking through some old notes from a speech given by Sam Southard years ago. He had talked about anger, which, he said, is always tied to the fear of losing something. When we become angry, we are defending something which we fear will be taken away. Southard urged us to get in touch with what we were defending.

His words were like a sunrise for me. I began to see that what I was defending was not my integrity but the level of comfort for which I had worked so long. The truth was, I enjoyed my possessions. They had become integral to my self-image. It was not the criticism of a few people that made me angry; it was the fear of losing my "investment."

In a word, I discovered that I had been "sucked back into the sponge of materialism." I had begun my ministry by storing up treasures in heaven and had ended up storing them on earth.

The question is: How do we prevent this process from recurring over and over again? Jesus gives us an answer, in the form of a mini-parable found in the next three verses of our study (Matt. 6:22–24). "The eye is the lamp of the body," he says, "If your eye is single, your whole body will be lighted. But if your eye is evil, your whole body will be dark. Therefore, if the light in you is dark, the darkness will be overwhelming." And then he adds, "No one can serve two masters; for he will hate one and love the other . . . You cannot serve God and the material."

He's telling us that keeping ourselves from lapsing back into materialism is a matter of "seeing" things in the right perspective. It's a matter of keeping our eye focused on the right object. *The "right object" is the eternal kingdom of God, which cannot rot or cease to exist.*

If we focus on what is *eternally* durable, our whole being (body) will be flooded with a sense of the eternal; that is, we will not reserve part of our lives for the worship of the material and part for the worship of God. If we attempt to focus on the world *and* the kingdom at the same time, our whole vision will become distorted. In other words, we can keep from falling into materialism only if we reduce our vision to a singular focus.

In verse 23 the word *evil* comes from the same root as the word *pornographic.* So "if your eye be pornographic, your whole outlook will be pornographic."

At base, pornography is a distortion of the real. The Christian objection to pornography should not be based *merely* upon the fact that it exhibits nakedness or explicit sex. It should be based upon the fact that it distorts the purpose and meaning of the human body and of sex. A movie is pornographic if it misrepresents the real nature and purpose of sex—or of anything else, actually.

Jesus is saying that an attempt to focus upon the kingdom and the world at the same time is pornographic. It distorts our entire perception. That is exactly what had happened to me in the process I described earlier. Somewhere along the line my single vision had become double vision. I had begun to think that I could store up treasures on earth *as well as* treasures in heaven. The result was a "pornographic view of reality."

While there was nothing wrong with bettering the material well-being of my family, there was everything wrong with trying to protect it at the cost of my ministry. My whole perspective as a servant in the kingdom had become darkened by my passion to retain material luxury. This experience taught me to regard all future criticism of my material status as a gift rather than a threat.

Let's summarize this discussion. How do we prevent being sucked back into the sponge of materialism? By focusing singularly upon what really counts, upon that which cannot be destroyed—the eternal kingdom of God. Focusing upon both the eternal *and* the corruptible (the material) is impossible. Trying to is pornographic; it distorts our entire perception. And trying to serve both God and the material only results in our resenting one and loving the other, which means we will live in a constant tension between the two. That kind of existence is pure misery. It does God no good, the world no good, us no good.

Here's another way to say it: "With one eye you can see the Forever." We can keep "the Forever"—the eternal kingdom of God—in focus only if our vision remains singular, if we see with only "one eye." In a word, Jesus is saying, "Let the kingdom be your single point of focus, and the kingdom will light your entire being. Split your focus and your entire being will be darkened." Distorted values stem from distorted vision.

We began this section by asking the question of how we can avoid being drawn back into materialism after experiencing the kingdom. We have answered that we must reduce our vision of the real to the kingdom. We must not lapse into thinking that we can serve both the kingdom which is eternal and the material which is transient. The kingdom must be our only focus.

But this answer only begs another question. How can the Christian know that he is focusing singularly upon the kingdom? Materialism is subtle, as we have noted. It creeps into our lives in such a way that we can be worshiping the material while thinking we are worshiping the eternal.

Ernest Campbell tells of looking up a couple, at the request of a friend, while he was on vacation at an island resort. He was overwhelmed by the magnificence of the couple's estate—a huge house, manicured lawn, two sleek limousines in the garage, a yacht moored to an attractive dock. The doorbell was answered by a butler, who ushered Campbell into an opulent sitting room. In a few minutes, an elegant, gracious lady entered to greet him. She began by apologizing for keeping him waiting. "We always call our daughter in California on Friday night," she said, "it is our one extravagance."[4]

Materialism can slip up on us unawares. We can come to accept our affluence as being ordinary and par for the course. *How can we tell whether we are actually storing up treasures in heaven or just kidding ourselves?* Jesus addresses this question in the next section on wealth (Matt. 6:25–34).

The Ulcer Issues

The gist of Jesus' message is this: if you want to find out whether you're worshiping God or the material, look at what worries you the most. What's causing you the most anxiety? What are the "ulcer issues" of your life?

Anxiety is peculiar to us humans. As far as we can

tell, no other creature is capable of it. The lower animals follow the cycles and demands of nature. They do not live in anticipation of death. Only man is capable of "standing outside himself" and seeing himself as a being on his way toward death. As the philosophers put it, man is the only creature who can see himself as a subject and an object at the same time.

The awareness of our tentative existence is the root cause of our anxiety. We worry because lurking in our subconscious minds is the knowledge that at any moment we could cease to be.

So our fear of death is a basic cause of worry. But there is another cause which is related to it. We are not only aware of the possibility of death; we are also aware of the possibility of eternal life. *In short, we know what we are—mortal creatures—and at the same time, we know what we can be—immortal creatures.* This means that all worry is caused by the fear of ceasing to exist without becoming what we can be.

Every human worry can be traced back to this basic anxiety. The person who is worried about his health is really concerned about dying before he can become what he wants to be. He doesn't want the clock to run out before he achieves his dream.

The person who is worried about his teenager's bad behavior is really concerned about two things: he, the parent, has failed to become what he could have been; and the child is destroying his own chances to become what he can be.

The anxiety which is caused by guilt also applies here. When we have either done wrong or failed to do right, why do we feel guilty? Because we know that we have failed to become what we know we can be.

The same applies to the worries which are related to material possessions. We worry over the acquisition of things, or over the loss of them, because, as I have noted several times, we live in a society which measures the worth of the self by the size of the financial statement. *We can't separate becoming the self we were meant to be from becoming rich!* As someone has said, "In this country, immortality and affluence mean the same thing!"

We worry about wealth or the lack of it because it tells us whether or not we are human! Remember Tillich's statement: We touch more and more things in order to determine whether we are real, not to determine whether the things are! We have been convinced that if we lose our things, we lose ourselves.

There is a beer commercial which says, "If you take away my Schlitz, you take away my gusto." That's the common notion regarding wealth: "If you take away my wealth, you take away my very being!"

Now, perhaps, we can hear Jesus' words about worry and wealth. "Stop worrying about your physical needs," he says. "After all, isn't life more than food and clothes? God feeds the birds; aren't you more than birds? God clothes the lilies with beautiful blossoms; aren't you more than lilies? Where's your faith? God knows your material needs; he will meet them. Since you're going to worry about something, worry about the kingdom and about what the kingdom requires of you! The material things you need will be added to you."

Have we ever really heard Jesus? Do we really believe that life is more than food and clothes and wealth? Well, look at the ulcer issues! What's your chief worry in life?

Do we really believe that life consists in being "more than birds and lilies"? In our culture, it is a mark of distinction to be "birds," to fly to far-off places, and especially in one's own customized airplane. Staying home is zero; walking and running are only for those who want to lose weight; driving is for the less privileged. But flying . . . ah! It is the mark of him who has arrived! Do we really believe that we are more than birds?

And what about "lilies"? How much do we worry about maintaining our beauty and vitality? Self-worth and beauty are almost synonymous in our society. Studies have shown that beautiful children have a far greater chance of "succeeding" in life than ugly children. For example, school teachers tend to trust a handsome child more readily than they do an ugly child. The nursery stories we heard as children carried the message that good is beautiful and bad is ugly. Remember the Ugly Duckling, the Princess and the Frog, Cinderella?

See the forty-year-old woman standing in front of the mirror on Monday morning. She's no longer the sweetheart of Sigma Chi. Gravity has tugged inexorably at her youth. She bought everything that Farrah and Cheryl suggested, but her husband still ran the grocery cart into the canned beans because he was staring at that sweet young thing at Safeway. He dyed his hair, traded in the station wagon for an MG, bought himself some open-collared silk shirts, a tiger-claw amulet, sunglasses, and a girdle to go under those tight continental pants with no pockets. And the "sweet young thing" stared back at him!

"Birds and lilies"—do we really believe that we amount to more than these? Why then are we getting ulcers from trying to be like them?

Do we also believe that God will provide his children with basic material necessities? Why then is there so much tension over money in our homes?

Once, in a church service where I was guest preacher, a prominent banker was giving the invocation. In the midst of his prayer, a young man started shouting.

"Listen to him!" he raved, "That —— hypocrite! He's the biggest fraud in town!"

For a moment, the congregation sat there with mouths agape. Then two ushers dragged the raving youngster out of the building. Later I learned that the boy was the banker's son! He had always been a quiet and polite boy, respected by everyone. Therefore, the general feeling was that he'd suddenly "popped a cork."

I went to the banker's home and sat for a long time talking to the lad. He was filled with shame at his outburst. Finally, he said, "Dr. Mann, I just couldn't take it any more. At church, Dad is always the model of Christian concern and faith. He speaks of how Jesus is the most valuable thing in the world. But at home, he and Mom argue constantly about bills and debts and wasting money. He gives me cars and clothes and trips, and then he gripes about my lack of appreciation for the value of a dollar."

And then the boy added, "He has an ulcer, you know; his stomach is like a sieve. I guarantee you it's because he's constantly worried about how he's going to keep us from wasting his fortune!"

"What's grinding your guts?" It's a good question to put to those who are trying to tell whether they are storing riches on earth or riches in heaven.

Jesus rests his case upon the question of faith. In our earlier discussion about the model prayer, we noted that the key issue governing our requests is this: Do we really trust that God has enough in his storehouse to meet our basic needs? The same issue is involved here. If we trust God to provide us with the basic necessities, we will not be worried about wealth. Anxiety over material things is a symptom of faithlessness. Our tendency is to protest this assertion. We keep saying, "Let's be realistic; we cannot avoid worry over material things. As Sophie Tucker said, 'I've been rich and I've been poor, and rich is better.'"

In a word, we try to water down Jesus' words about wealth, just as we try to soften the other commands of the Sermon. We have convinced ourselves that it is impossible not to worry about material things. But we fail to realize that our arguments stem from the fact that we have *already sold our souls* to materialism! Our arguments are much like those of the habitual user who argues for the legalization of marijuana! We plead that Jesus' commands are too rigid, because we're already breaking them!

Summary

We have said that Jesus had some ideas about wealth which were unnerving both to his contemporaries and to us moderns. His ideas, however, were not based upon the notion that it is a sin to be rich. Worshiping material possessions is not peculiar to the rich alone; it is the sin of all who would judge their self-worth by the amount of their wealth. It is the sin of "thingification"— of turning away from God and looking to things in order to find fulfillment in life.

This basic way of looking at life's meaning can be called "being had by what you have." When the self is sold to the material, it dies with the material.

It is human nature to store up for the future. All such saving is ultimately designed to secure the self against all threats. In short, all preserving is a desire for immortality. Therefore, the only way to keep from being had by what we have is to "save for a sunny day," to stake our lives on the eternal kingdom of God. That is the only saving which will save us eternally.

However, we cannot believe this until we have had a glimpse of the kingdom. Until we have been "touched by the eternal" through Jesus Christ, we shall only stake our destinies on the material.

But how do we keep from being sucked back into the sponge of materialism once we have had a foretaste of the kingdom? We must constantly focus our entire efforts on the kingdom. We cannot serve God and material things at the same time. Double vision leads to complete blindness.

And how can we tell whether we are indeed focusing singularly upon the kingdom? The answer lies in our worries. What causes us the most anxiety—our material well-being or our effectiveness as agents for the kingdom?

The heart of the matter is this: *either we believe that our security rests with God's ability to give us fulfillment, or we believe in our own ability to fulfill ourselves through accumulation of material things.* Either we trust God, or we trust mammon for life. It's neither a sin to be rich nor a sin to be poor. It's a sin to allow wealth to determine what we're staking our lives on.

QUESTIONS FOR STUDY

1. Did Jesus teach that it is a sin to be rich?
2. What does the term *thingification* mean?
3. What was Jesus' advice on how to keep from being "had by what we have"?
4. What lies behind our human inclination to accumulate material possessions? Do we want material things or something else? What is it we really want?

5. How does a Christian avoid being sucked back into materialism once he has glimpsed the kingdom of God?

6. How can a Christian tell whether he's focusing his life on eternal values?

CHAPTER FIVE

UNNERVING NOTIONS ABOUT WHERE A CHRISTIAN LIVES

(Matthew 7:1–27)

The Man in the Middle

I have tried to show throughout this book that the Sermon on the Mount is based upon Jesus' concept of the kingdom of God. In the introduction I gave a sketch as to the meaning of the kingdom. It is necessary to review and expand this concept now, for unless we understand it we cannot hear the final segment of the sermon which is contained in Matthew 7.

First, the kingdom of God is God's reign over any community or any person who acknowledges him as king. Second, the kingdom has existed in three stages throughout history:

(1) *The kingdom was.* When God created humans, he was acknowledged as king. But humans were created with the freedom to reject God's reign, and they did. The lordship of the earth was therefore turned over to the human race. However, God continued to try to woo us back to himself. That's what the entire biblical history is about—God's efforts to regain our allegiance by revealing himself to a people, Israel, and by commissioning them to be his agents for bringing back the kingdom.

(2) *The kingdom is.* When Israel failed to carry out her commission, God entered the world in the person of Jesus Christ. Therefore, the kingdom has been re-established. It is here now! Every person and every community which has accepted Jesus is already a member of the kingdom, and is an agent of the kingdom.

(3) *But the kingdom in its fullness is yet to be.* A day will come when God's reign will be acknowledged universally. This means that the Christian has only partially experienced the kingdom. He's had a foretaste, an

appetizer, of what is yet to come. In short, he lives between the times—between the dawn of the kingdom in Jesus and the sunrise of the kingdom in the future. He is "the man in the middle," so to speak. He belongs partially to this world and partially to the next.

This chapter is about living in the middle, and *that* means tension! As the old rural preacher once said, "Life may be hell, but the Christian life is 'hellier'!" To be a Christian means to live in tension between the now and the not yet. Living in the middle *means that the rewards for living the Christian life are delayed rewards.*

Throughout the Sermon we have kept running into this hard truth. When we looked at happiness, we had to admit that, although we can have *some* happiness now, full happiness lies in the future. We saw in chapter 2 that going beyond the law will not reap instant benefits; in fact, it will more likely bring us discomfort and pain. Practicing piety for God's sake was the theme of chapter 3. This kind of piety doesn't benefit *us* in this world, but only in the world to come. In the preceding chapter on wealth, the same holds true. Storing up treasures in heaven will not provide us material comfort now.

If we want to pinpoint what it is that *really* makes the Sermon on the Mount X-rated, it is this recurring notion that *the Christian has to wait for his rewards.* That's the real crunch of Jesus' message: "You can't have it all now; you have to wait. You have to live in the middle, between what is and what is yet to be!"

That's a repulsive idea to many of us, because we don't want to wait! We don't want to live in the middle! We want happiness *now!* We want the rewards of being salt and light *now!* We want praise for our piety *now!* We want material comfort *now!*

Several years ago, a movie entitled *The Loved One* was released. It was a satire on the funeral business.

Jonathan Winters portrayed the "Reverend Glen-worthy," the mogul of a complete "death service" which included embalming, caskets, interment, and cremation. The cemetery had underwater plots for those who had spent their lives in aquatic endeavors, a simulated construction site for those who were in the building business, a hospital-like crypt for those in the medical profession, and so on.

The crisis came when the cemetery began to run out of space. Something had to be done to "get rid of all those stiffs and make room for some more," as Glen-worthy put it. He hit upon a novel idea. He would provide his customers with a "burial rocket." They would be placed in the nose cone and launched into space.

The idea worked! The government, the military, and the clients went for it. The movie ends with a corpse being launched into space while the President of the United States and assorted dignitaries stand with hands over hearts. Cannons boom, and a band plays. The last line of the movie is delivered by Rev. Glenworthy. With a mystic, triumphant countenance, he looks to heaven and shouts, "Resurrection Now" as the rocket thunders into the clouds.

I saw that movie three times, because I believe it reflects the essence of our rejection of Jesus' message throughout the centuries. We want "resurrection now," but we cannot have it if we take discipleship seriously. For being a disciple means living with one foot on earth and the other in heaven. The Christian is the man in the middle.

The Middle Is the Narrow Way

I believe that all of the teachings in the final section of the Sermon (Matt. 7:1–27) are designed to illustrate the theme stated above. In a word, they are examples of how the Christian is to be the man in the middle.

The key to the entire chapter is contained in verses 13–14: "Go through the narrow gate; for the way that leads to destruction is wide and broad, and there are many who travel it. But the way that leads to life is narrow and hard, and there are few who find it."

Traditionally, we have interpreted Jesus' words as meaning that the Christian is to take a rigid stance on one side of an issue—a stance which separates him from the world's position. In other words, the "narrow way" has been viewed as a way of narrow dogmatism, the Christian's duty is to stand for the absolute right against the absolute wrong.

I do not believe that this was Jesus' idea at all! On the contrary, a close look at Matthew 7 reveals that *the Christian way is the way of moderation.* "The narrow way" is that thin line between truth and error, right and wrong, liberal and conservative, rigidity and permissiveness.

For instance, consider the fact that the most difficult place to stand on any issue is in the middle. It's easy to take one side or the other, but if one tries to stand between the two and do justice to both, he is scorned and rejected by those on either side.

Carlyle Marney died two weeks before I began writing this book. He was one of the most perceptive and creative Southern Baptists of our time. However, it is tragic that he was considered a theological renegade by the majority of his own denomination. He was invited to lecture at Harvard and Yale; he filled the pulpit at Riverside Church, New York; his books were read the world over; but he was virtually hounded out of his "own country."

His problem was that he defied all of the convenient labels. He irked the conservatives by quoting Harnack,

Schweitzer, and others who would question the infallible inspiration of the Scriptures; he rankled the liberals by insisting that the Bible is the only rule of faith.

Marney's last book, *Priests to Each Other,* is one of the most exciting interpretations of what it means to be a Christian in the modern world that I have ever read. Anyone who reads it cannot help but see that Marney was a deeply spiritual man. But his downfall was that he believed in all truth regardless of who spoke it, and at the same time he believed none of it *completely.* For instance, listen to what he wrote about the church:

> We Christians have been given a mighty weapon—the conviction that the man Christ can make us whole, and that men who are being made whole can create a well society aiming to keep the world out and to bring the world in. The Christian church has been a failure at both. We have neither kept the worldliness out nor have we brought the world in. Relevant Christianity . . . demands a new priesthood: a priesthood that believes in the redemption of the world, not the redemption of the church.[1]

This quote gets to the heart of why men like Marney are without honor in their own countries. They are "men in the middle." They try to travel the narrow way between absolutism, listening to all but casting their lots totally with none. Whether the field is ethical behavior, dogmatics, politics, or any other, the loneliest position of all is in the middle.

And yet *that* is precisely the place where Jesus calls us to live as his disciples. Martin Luther King tried to steer a middle course in human justice, rejecting violence on the one hand and a system of racial tyranny on the other. He had no patience with either white racists or black racists. And his was a lonely position.

Lincoln tried to steer the middle course between endorsing slavery and punishing the South after slavery was defeated—a lonely stance.

And Jesus himself was the man in the middle. He angered them all before he was through. The rigid Pharisees didn't want him, even though he upheld the Law. The Sadducees didn't want him, even though he made the Law flexible. The Zealots didn't want him, even though he talked about revolution. The Romans didn't want him, even though he preached obedience to Caesar. His problem was that he accepted some of the truth from everyone, but all of the truth from no one. The narrow way is the middle way, which attempts "to bring the world in and keep worldliness out."

Between Judging and Accepting

As we said, every subject Jesus treats in Matthew 7 illustrates the tension of living in the middle. His first illustration has to do with steering a middle course between *judging and accepting* the behavior of others. In verses 1–5 he tells us not to condemn, but in verse 6 he tells us not to give "what is holy to dogs" or to "cast our pearls before swine."

Many have felt that verse 6 is so out of step with verses 1–5 that it must have been added to the text later by someone who couldn't tolerate Jesus' instructions against judging. But I think verse 6 is in keeping with Jesus' whole argument. He's telling us that our task is to judge a person's deeds without judging the person. We may refuse to condone a person's deeds—indeed, we may condemn his deeds—but we must not condemn the person; we must not reject him and separate ourselves from him.

In short, Jesus tells us to live in that narrow place

between rejecting deeds and rejecting persons, to walk the narrow line between judging and accepting!

This is the loneliest, the most difficult place of all to live. To reject a person's deeds without playing the role of judge (God) is foreign to our common way of thinking. Throughout Christian history we have been unwilling to love people unless their deeds are "loveable." We want to be God. We want to prescribe punishment for others.

As we noted in our discussion of love for enemies, Jesus commands us to do away with evil, but to salvage the evildoers. But this idea makes us nervous. We seem to be unable to distinguish between condemning evil and condemning persons. I have often said that many so-called Christians would be gravely disappointed if, on the final day of judgment, God were to let everybody off scot-free. For they live with a constant need to see people punished for their sins. There is a certain sadism built into the kind of religion which longs for retribution. The very mention of the possibility of universal forgiveness sets off a Pavlovian reaction among some of the most active religionists I know.

We must stand against what false prophets teach and do; we cannot cast the holy truth and the precious pearls of the kingdom before "dogs" and "swine." But we must not persecute and do harm to the false prophets themselves!

When shall we learn that the answer to a false doctrine is not the punishment of its teacher, but a better doctrine? In the early days of Christian history, the Church placed one Nestorius on trial because he was teaching an unorthodox view of the nature of Christ. At the trial, he presented his views in a spirit of humility, asking to be corrected for his errors by anyone who could give him a reasonable alternative. No

alternatives were given; Nestorius was summarily condemned and burned at the stake!

The same fate befell John Huss, Feliz Mantz, Ser-
vetus, Savanarola, and a host of other so-called heretics.
Instead of answering their doctrines with better doctrines and keeping them in the community, the church
"wasted" them.

There is a narrow middle ground between accepting
and judging. It's neither heroic nor easy, and few there
are who live there. But it is the place to which Jesus has
called us to live.

However, this raises a serious question. How can we
live in the middle, between accepting and judging?
How can we reject another's lifestyle without rejecting
him? I probably sound like a broken record, but I
believe the answer lies in seeing others as part of
ourselves. Only if we can avoid viewing others as
"theys," as aliens, can we keep from condemning them.

When someone teaches or does something which we
think is wrong, we must remember that we ourselves
possess the same "wrongness" in our being. Perhaps we
are wrong on a different subject, but we are wrong, too!
Will Rogers said, "Everyone's ignorant, 'cept on different subjects." Everyone's a sinner, 'cept on different
subjects, too!

Isn't this what Jesus is getting at when he says, "Why
do you condemn the speck in your brother's eye and
pay no attention to the log in your own?" We cannot
play God and condemn others if we are aware that we
deserve the same condemnation. If we know that we
deserve judgment, we won't dare judge others. Jesus
put it this way: "He who is without sin, let him cast the
first stone" (John 8:7).

The Christian is called to live between the times—
between what is and what is yet to be. Applied to the

issue of judging others, this means that he is called to live between condemning a person's deeds and condemning the person as unworthy to be a part of the kingdom of God. That's a lonely place to live.

Between Asking and Receiving from God

Now, Jesus gives a second illustration of living in the middle by addressing the subject of receiving what we ask from God. Some would confine his words to prayer only, but I believe his intention is much broader. He's not only talking about how God answers prayer, but about how he fulfills our quests for all truth and justice and love.

The point is that the Christian must live in that obscure no man's land between partial fulfillment and ultimate fulfillment. He must learn to be content with uncertainties. He must walk most of the time by faith and not by sight. In a word, he must learn to get by on glimpses rather than on full visions.

All of the verbs in this portion of our text (Matt. 7:7–11), are in the *future* tense: "Ask and you *will* receive"—not immediately, but in the future. "Seek and you *will* find, knock and the door *will be* opened to you." All that we said in the first section of this chapter applies here. The full rewards of the kingdom are *delayed rewards*. There's no such thing as absolute truth, absolute blessing, or absolute answer to prayer when it comes to receiving from God all that we want.

I took lessons from a famous golf teacher who resides in our city. He is now bent with age, a wisp of a man with snow-white hair and humorous blue eyes. He's a bit of an imp.

After adjusting my grip and swing, he had me hitting the ball farther and straighter than I had imagined possible. I drove a three-wood 210 yards to a practice green, and the ball stopped six inches from the cup. I turned triumphantly to the old pro and said, "Now, what was wrong with *that!*" "It didn't go in the hole," he said.

It's that way with receiving what we want from God. We can get close, occasionally, but we can't get it in the cup. This is the agony of the life of faith. We must be content to live without full vision, without "full" fulfillment.

I get very suspicious whenever I hear someone who claims that every step he takes in life is taken on direct orders from God. I suppose it's because God has never dealt with me in that way. I think it was Elton Trueblood who said that he was a "reverent agnostic" whom God always forced to act on the basis of uncertain evidence. The same has always been true for me.

There have been only four times in my twenty-year Christian pilgrimage in which I can truthfully say beyond a doubt that God gave me indisputable orders. The rest of the time, he has always forced me to take the leap of faith.

The Bible says that without faith it is impossible to please God (Heb. 11:6). If we received every time we asked, if we found every time we sought, if the door of absolute truth were opened every time we knocked, we wouldn't even need faith!

We Christians must live in the narrow middle between doubt and certainty. And sometimes all that keep us from giving in to doubt entirely are those few glimpses which God has given us of the kingdom.

I remember Tiny, a frail woman—four-foot-ten. Her husband was killed, leaving her with four children, one of whom was blind. Tiny supported them with two jobs, and had them in worship every Sunday. Then her sighted daughter contracted leukemia. For five years I heard Tiny pray, while the painful disease ravaged the child. Tiny bore her pain and suffering privately.

As her daughter lay dying, I asked her how she could still believe. Did she have some special sustaining sense of God's presence? "God?" she said, "Why no! I haven't been aware of his being around here in years. He could be ten thousand miles away for all I know! But he's here, all right. I know it, because I got a faint glimpse of him one time when I was eighteen years old."

The faith to live between asking and receiving, seeking and finding . . . the faith to live with uncertainty . . . the faith to keep on keeping on, with minimal evidence—that's what living in the middle is all about.

Do we really believe that God will answer our seeking in some future time? Can we stand the tension of the obscure middleground between seeking and finding? If we can, why do we keep trying to have it all *now?* Why do we keep trying to circumvent faith and come up with absolute systems?

I suspect it's because Jesus' words unnerve us. They are too explosive and harsh for us to tolerate. We don't want the agony of living in the middle, between asking and receiving.

Between Asking and Receiving from Men

If the Christian is to live between requesting and receiving what he wants from God, it follows that he must do the same thing with reference to what he wants from his fellow-man. This principle is contained in Matthew 7:12, the saying of Jesus which we call "The Golden Rule."

Literally, the verse reads, "Whatever it is you want from men, do this to them." What do we really want from others? Love, esteem, fairness, honesty, acceptance, good will—that pretty much covers it. If that's what we want, that's what we should give, says Jesus.

But this is where the problem comes in. For we all know that when we give these things to others, we seldom receive them in return! We've learned from experience that it doesn't pay to give love and good will indiscriminately. To give love is to make oneself vulnerable. To give love to another is to give him the power to hurt us and control us. That's dangerous business.

We don't want to place ourselves in the weak position that giving to others places us. Nevertheless, Jesus calls us to live between giving our love to others and receiving the reward of loving in the world to come.

In short, the Golden Rule is a call to live in the middle—to give love without receiving love, to be honest without being treated honestly, to be fair without being treated fairly, to accept without being accepted.

Jesus, we wish you hadn't said that! We don't want to live in the middle. If we love, we want to be loved back, *now!* As we often say, "We cannot live without love." That is true, but the Christian already has love—the love of God! He doesn't have to be rewarded for his love by men.

This brings us to the real reason many people cannot live in the middle when it comes to loving. They cannot love men without being loved by men, because they haven't experienced God's love. The only way we can give to men without receiving is to know that we are loved by God. "We love others because he first loved us," says Paul.

He doesn't mean that we humans love other humans only because God loves us. He means that we *Christians* can love others without being loved in return because God loves us. Human love requires reciprocation. Any human can love if he's loved in return. But only the Christian can love without being loved in return. And that's because he has experienced God's love.

Thus, the Christian who is called to live between times, between the world as it is and the world as it is yet to be, must also be content to live between asking and receiving, between wanting and getting. It's an X-rated place to live, and few are those who reside there.

Between Doing and Believing

Jesus finished the Sermon with another illustration of the "man in the middle." Actually, he is addressing the age-old question of faith and works. Does a Christian get into the kingdom by believing right, or by doing right? Some say one, some say the other.

I don't wish to write a theological treatise on the subject at this point; I only wish to express what Jesus teaches in Matthew 7:15–27. And my opinion is that he points us toward the same tension he's been expressing all along. *A Christian is called to live between faith and works.* He cannot enter the kingdom by merely believing, nor can he enter by merely doing. He must hold both in tension. To use Jesus' words, he must "hear and do." He must believe (the word translated "hear" means "hear and believe"), and he must act on what he believes.

That this is true can be seen by examining the text. In verses 15–20, Jesus tells his disciples to evaluate religious teachers by the fruit they bear. If they proclaim great truths but bear no fruit—that is, *do* nothing to increase the kingdom—they are false prophets. Entrance into the kingdom depends on doing.

However, in verses 22–23, Jesus reverses the idea. "Many will come to me in the last day and show me their mighty works: prophecy, casting out demons, and other powerful deeds. And I shall say to them, depart from me, you whose works were lawless." Entrance into the kingdom depends on believing.

The point is that works are useless without faith and vice versa. The parable of the two housebuilders points this out (verses 24–27). Those who try to believe without doing or to do without believing are like the man who builds his house upon the sand. But those who hold believing and doing together in tension are like the man who builds his house upon a rock. It cannot be destroyed.

We must live between doing and believing, and that also is an X-rated idea in the Christian community. Some of us would prefer to reduce our duties to a matter of believing the right number of religious propositions. There's great convenience in making Christianity a "head-trip." It allows us to define all our obligations, print them in a creed, and say "I believe." Then we don't have *to do* anything!

I once attended a funeral service for a man who had been a known figure of the underworld. He had been convicted for murder, trafficking in drugs, and running a prostitution ring. The minister said, "Now we all know that Gus had his ups and downs, but I believe that he is in heaven at this very moment. For at the tender age of nine he accepted Jesus as his Lord and Savior during a vacation Bible school in this very church. No matter what he did later in life, his soul was secured in heaven from the moment he believed."

Perhaps Gus *is* in heaven—how would I know? I'm not God, and such matters are his business. Perhaps the minister needed to say what he did in order to give hope and comfort to Gus's family. I too believe that we should always sound a note of hope. But I do not accept that Gus entered the kingdom because he had believed a given number of truths at one time and in one place. We cannot get into the kingdom merely because our theological head is straight! The Bible says that even the devils are quite orthodox (James 2:19)!

On the other hand, there are some who would prefer to reduce discipleship to doing. What one believes doesn't matter; it's what he does that counts. This group tends to regard intellectuals as "pointy-heads," and disdains all efforts to make religion reasonable. Ironically, they quite often use a great deal of logic to refute those who would make Christianity logical!

Little do they realize that all doing is based upon some kind of logical system of thought. We all live our daily lives according to a world-view which was at one time worked out by someone we've never heard of nor would probably understand if we did! For example, most of the people living in Russia today wouldn't understand Marx if they read him, but they live by his philosophy. Neither would most Americans understand Rousseau, or Locke, or Dewey, but our values have been shaped by them.

I'm trying to say that what we believe *is* important. In Christian terms, what we believe about God, and man, and the world, and salvation is as important as what we do. For what we do will be determined by what we believe, just as what we believe will be proved by what we do.

The easy way, the way that is wide and broad, the way which leads to destruction is the way of doing without believing or believing without doing. But the narrow way which leads to life is the middle way of *doing and believing*.

Albert Schweitzer left material security and fame to spend his life healing sick men and women the rest of the world ignored. Could anyone fault a man like Schweitzer? Well, think about this: He said that Jesus was a good man, but a deluded apocalyptic Jew who thought he was the Messiah but wasn't. Schweitzer also taught reverence for all life. He wouldn't so much as squash a roach or an ant that was trying to crawl onto his plate. But he killed germs by the millions!

Schweitzer's "doing" exceeded that of most men who ever lived. God grant that we would all follow his example. But, what of his "believing"? *Why* did he do what he did? I would wager that it was not for the sake of some deluded apocalyptic Jew!

Do you begin to feel the rub of Jesus' ideas now? Do you catch why they make us nervous? It's because they come crashing through all of our rosy illusions! They burst our sense of decency and respect.

I chose Schweitzer as an illustration because no man in his century has commanded more reverence than he. He stands near the top of every opinion poll designed to determine the greatest personalities of our time. He stands at the top of mine too! To question the sanctity of a man like that blows my mind!

Yet here comes Jesus saying that believing is as important as doing. Neither mighty faith nor mighty works qualify us for the kingdom—we must live in tension between the two. And that idea is rated X to most of us!

Summary

In this chapter we have tried to lay out Jesus' answer to the question of where a Christian is to live. Theologically speaking, the Christian lives "between the times," between the dawn of God's kingdom on earth and its consummation which is yet to come. In other words, the Christian is the "man in the middle." He is part of the world and part of the kingdom of God. The rewards for his labors are delayed. He cannot "have it all" now.

In practical terms, this means that the Christian's life is tentative. Not only must he live without absolute rewards; he must also live without absolute knowledge and direction. The narrow way which he is to follow is the way of the middle. He must live between truth and error, right and wrong, rigidity and permissiveness.

Jesus illustrates what "living in the middle" means in his teachings about judging, asking God and others for what we want, and believing and doing. When it comes to judging others, living in the middle means rejecting another's deeds but accepting him. When it comes to getting what we want from God and man, living in the middle means giving ourselves without receiving full measure in return. And when it comes to believing and doing, living in the middle means doing both—that is, holding faith and works in tension.

The unnerving notions of Jesus in this chapter as well as the others are yet to be tried on a wide scale, even though we have had them at our disposal for two thousand years. I suspect Kierkegaard was close to the truth when he said: "The Christianity of the New Testament simply does not exist. Instead, millions of people through the centuries have cunningly sought little by little to cheat God out of Christianity, and have succeeded in making Christianity exactly the opposite of what it is in the New Testament."[2]

But if ever Jesus' unnerving ideas were to become the norm—better still, *when they do become the norm!*—so, shall the kingdom come. Even so, come Lord Jesus!

QUESTIONS FOR STUDY

1. What does it mean to "live in the middle"?
2. How does the idea of "living in the middle" relate to the biblical concept of the kingdom of God?
3. What does living in the middle have to do with judging others? With asking and receiving from God? With asking and receiving from our fellow-man? With faith and works?

NOTES

Introduction

1. Ernest T. Campbell, "On Living Out of Phase," sermon (New York: National Radio Pulpit, June 1973), pp. 43–48.
2. Otto Riethmueller, "The City and the Mount," *The Student World* 30 (1937):203.
3. See Amos N. Wilder, "The Sermon on the Mount," *The Interpreter's Bible*, 12 vols. (New York: Abingdon Press, 1951) 7:160–161.
4. Ibid., p. 157.
5. Ibid., p. 157.

Chapter One

1. "Happiness in America," *Psychology Today*, June 1977, pp. 38–44.
2. Alexander Solzhenitsyn, "The West's Decline in Courage," *Wallstreet Journal*, 13 June 1978, p. 1.
3. Helmut Thielicke, *Between Heaven and Earth*, trans. John W. Doberstein (New York: Harper and Row, 1965), pp. 183–189.
4. Dietrich Bonhoeffer, *Letters and Papers from Prison* (London: Collins Fontana Books, 1960), p. 94.
5. George Buttrick, quoted in William E. Hull, "The Ordeal of the Ministry," sermon (Louisville, Kentucky: Crescent Hill Baptist Church, 4 October 1970), p. 1.
6. Harry Emerson Fosdick, *Dear Mr. Brown* (New York: Harper and Row, 1961), p. 97.
7. Ibid., p. 100.
8. Victor Hugo, quoted in Harry Emerson Fosdick, *Living Under Tension* (New York: Harper and Row, 1941), p. 180.

9. Henry David Thoreau, "Life Without Principle," *The Writing of Thoreau,* ed. Brooks Atkinson (New York: The Modern Library, 1937), p. 716.
10. Sören Kierkegaard, *Purity of Heart,* trans. Douglas V. Steere (New York: Harper and Brothers, 1938), p. xiv.

Chapter Two

1. Solzhenitsyn, "The West's Decline," p. 1.
2. James Dobson, *Dare to Discipline* (Wheaton, Illinois: Tyndale House, 1974), pp. 168–169.

Chapter Three

1. Thomas C. Campbell and Yoshio Fukiyama, *The Fragmented Layman* (New York: Pilgrim Press, 1970), p. 222.

Chapter Four

1. Alan K. Campbell and Donna E. Shalala, "Problems Unsolved, Solutions Untried: The Urban Crisis," *The States and the Urban Crisis,* ed. Alan K. Campbell (New York: Columbia University Press, 1970), p. 3.
2. Dorothy Sayers, *Christian Letters to a Post Christian World* (Grand Rapids, Michigan: Wm. B. Eerdmans, 1969), p. 149.
3. Saul D. Alinsky, *Reveille for Radicals* (New York: Random House, 1946), p. 229.
4. Ernest T. Campbell, "On Giving Away the Sleeves of Our Vest," sermon (New York: Riverside Church, 14 November 1971), p. 6.

Chapter Five

1. Carlyle Marney, *Priests to Each Other* (Valley Forge: Judson Press, 1975), p. 9.
2. Sören Kierkegaard, *Attack on Christendom,* trans. Walter Lowrie (Princeton, New Jersey: Princeton University Press, 1944), pp. 32–33.